Becoming Real

Essays on the Teachings of a Master

Edited by
Alphonse and Rachel Goettmann

Translated by
Theodore J. Nottingham

Published by
Theosis Books
www.theosisbooks.com

ISBN 0-9664960-7-8
Cover art by Rebecca Nottingham

Printed in the United States of America.

Becoming Real
Essays on the Teachings of a Master

Table of Contents

BECOMING REAL

THE AUTHORS OF *BECOMING REAL*

GERHARD WEHR: writer, professor at Nuremberg, specialist in the history of religions, he has published several well known biographies, including those of C.G. Jung, Rudolf Steiner, and the primary biography of Karlfried Graf Durckheim.

JEAN AND GISELE MARCHAL: medical doctors, psychotherapists, students of Graf Durckheim.

BERNARD REROLLE: Catholic priest, professor of philosophy, member of the Forum-Vaugirard in Paris where he directs the studies of contemplative traditions and the encounter of Eastern and Western cultures and religions.

PIERRE ERNY: professor at the University of Human Sciences at Strasbourg.

WILLI MASSA: Orthodox priest, director of the Ecumenical Center "Exercitium Humanum" at Neumuhle.

ARNAUD DESJARDINS: Student of Hindu, Tibetan, Japanese and Sufi masters, he has written numerous works and heads an ashram at Vers-Pont-du-Gard.

JEAN-BAPTISTE LOTZ: German Jesuit, student of Heidegger, professor of philosophy and theology at the University of Munich and at the Gregorian University in Rome, author of many books.

BECOMING REAL

JACQUES BRETON: Catholic priest, hermit at Carmel, student of Graf Durckheim. Related to a Zen Buddhist monastery in Japan, he directs the Assise Center at Saint-Gervais en-Vexin.

JEAN-YVES LELOUP: Orthodox priest, doctorate in psychology, philosophy and theology.

ALPHONSE GOETTMANN: Orthodox priest, director of Bethanie, a Center for Spiritual Encounters near Metz and the author of several books on Durckheim.

PREFACE

by Theodore J. Nottingham

There have been many teachers of life-giving wisdom down through the ages. Each has left his or her mark on humanity, touching the lives of individuals in search of meaning. They have discovered and shared an awareness of reality which is timeless and utterly transforming. Like rare gems, they have each reflected aspects of cosmic truth whose glow has changed forever our understanding of ourselves and of the universe.

From this blessed line of teachers has come forth in our time yet another master. Karlfried Graf Durckheim, who died at the age of 92 in December of 1988, is a beacon for humanity whose influence has only begun to be felt. Here is a man who brought together the vision of Meister Eckhart, C. G. Jung, Zen Buddhism, and the spirituality of early Christianity. Out of his experience and understanding, he has created a new language for the practical transformation of human consciousness.

He speaks to us of our two natures, the essential and the existential; of daily life as an exercise for the breakthrough of eternal Being; of the body as an expression of the invisible; of our becoming transparent to the Transcendent. This is not a philosophy or a religion or a new kind of psychology. Karlfried Graf Durckheim teaches us

5

genuine, all consuming transformation, encompassing each moment of our lives. He uncovers the essence of religion as an encounter with the Holy and brings together the summits of Eastern and Western thought. The reader will find gathered in this book striking insights into Durckheim's wisdom from some of his closest students, people who are making their own mark on the spiritual evolution of humankind.

From a detailed biography to the tracing of the radical implications of the master's teaching, this work offers the keys to understanding not only Durckheim the man, but also the heart of sacred Scriptures, the application of Eastern practices, and the nature and purpose of humanity.

INTRODUCTION

by Alphonse and Rachel Goettmann

We have only one Master: "Jesus-Christ, the eternal Master" as Durckheim himself called him. It is written that "in many and various ways God spoke of old to our fathers by the prophets; but in these last days he has spoken to us by a Son," (Hebrews 1:1) and He still sends us messengers to open the way to Him. Graf Durckheim is one of these messengers. It matters little what we call them, for they are only the multiple faces of the One who is out of time. It is said of the disciple that when he is ready, the master arrives; that can be said of time as well: when it is dark and imprisoned in the horizontal dimension, then one day it cries toward the Transcendent. That day has arrived.

The last world war has slowly engendered it. Anguished by death and meaninglessness, humanity has risen out of it and has thrown itself by an instinct for survival into possessing, knowledge, power, overproduction. Such a person with the full stomach and the empty heart lacks nothing except happiness. This new market has been filled by sorcerers of well-being who have done great business. Already dreadfully sick, man is further lost in their illusory forms of "liberation." But these frail mirages will eventually disappear, leaving us with an even greater yearning. Just like the sysmic quivers of the planet, these cries from the depths of our being reveal layers which have been completely ignored. But these sediments of the human being, buried beneath the weight of cultures and civilizations, covered over by the artifice of centuries, are now entering into the light of our consciousness. The great convulsions of our times come from within us.

A voice cries from the core of our being. It is the call of the master. And this call announces new beginnings. But a change of humanity and of its consciousness always takes place in relation to its ancestral traditions. Only in returning to our first genesis can we find a way out of our current impasses, culling from our ancient treasures "that which eye has not seen, nor ear heard, nor the heart of man conceived, which God has prepared for those who love him." (John 5:17) But for this humanity "in the making" God has need of wisewomen and wisemen who assist us in being born into the "secret and hidden wisdom of God, which God decreed before the ages for our glorification" (1 Co 2:8). The person and work of Graf Durckheim is an answer to this call. Durckheim has contributed to this awakening as few others have in our time. He has done this on two levels: in the secret face to face encounter of the master and the disciple and in the general calling into question of the established system; these two are one and the same.

Whoever came near to him was struck by the fact that Durckheim did not close himself off into a role: he was himself, he was what he said and wrote. You felt in his presence a fullness, an intensity of attention which made you feel truly alive for the first time. Everything was centered in this relationship in which he became your confident, a companion on the way or your therapist. In this encounter, there was always a density of energy which gave way to the numinous and the inexpressible recognition of the One whom he called "the Great Third One." The silences between master and disciple would then become longer and sometimes Durckheim invited you to simply join him in meditation. Everyone felt unique around him. His blind eyes could pierce into the depths of your soul, as though scrutinizing the roots of your motives; or as though seeking to generate your ultimate decision without which there is no accomplishment. But in every case his gaze was filled with a love which was neither oppressive nor demanding. It seized your inner source, there where we can feel ourselves being reborn; the dialogue took place in your essence, as though all the walls had vanished. Someone else resonated within you, the very mystery of your being.

When Durckheim rose at the end of the interview and placed a hand vibrant with tenderness on your shoulder or put his hands on your head to bless you, a new joy and peace would invade your entire being. This revelation to oneself and to one's deep reality placed all one's behavior in a new light. You could be an expert in art, consider yourself advanced on the path or possess important knowledge. Yet at the first contact with Durckheim all of that crumbled, as though he had pulled the rug out from under you. The consciousness that you knew nothing was overwhelming! He who has passed through that experience knows what a treasure it is. This is how we recognize an authentic master and this is perhaps the greatest service he can render to the disciple at the beginning. The total loss of security, the surrendering of all foundations provokes a first awakening: the abyss opened within you creates an incredible feeling of freedom, then plunges you into another state of consciousness. You rub your eyes from a long sleep and all of your past studies will now reorganize themselves completely, transfigured by this transforming shock. You will then better understand the unconditional requirement

of Jesus to his disciples: "Go, sell all you have, and follow me" (Ga 5:22).

We can take nothing with us into the beyond. There can
only be a mutation of being. Freed from all conditioning,
these creative forces will now be able to go to work. The
enormous risk of acquired knowledge is always found in
easy satisfaction, imprisonment in one's possessions, or
falling asleep on one's laurels! Here the Path is work.
Those who approached Durckheim for recipes or techniques left with a new way of living. But to live is to
work for "to work is to live without dying" said Rilke in
agreement with all spiritual traditions. This is of course
work on oneself, progress on the Path, and there is nothing for which one should ever stop even for a moment.
The human spirit is absolute like the Spirit of God, and
as such it has no rest: its field of action is the twenty-four
hours of the day. Here is where the sorting occurs: there
is the one who indefinitely hesitates on the "path toward
the Path," doing exercises here and there in hopes of attaining wisdom one day without too much fatigue or
believing that he has already achieved it. And then there
is the one who is on the Path by virtue of an irrevocable
decision, giving to his being a unique and definitive
orientation which makes of every moment the best opportunity for moving forward.

He finds in everything he does a way to advance internally. This person no longer does exercises, he has himself
become exercise. His heart is pure, that is, outside of the
multiple. But he pays the price with his blood: "Give
your blood and receive the Spirit" states one of those
powerful sayings of the Desert Fathers. To be "on the
Path" is then synonymous with being a disciple. Durckheim was uncommonly intransigent on this point, though
with that indescribable love which so characterized him.
But once the disciple had reached the best part of him-

self, the master gave him his freedom. The requirement was fundamental: either the exercise became constant or there was, according to Durckheim, little to hope for. Amateurism leads nowhere and, as with every master, Durckheim did not waste his time with lazy souls. On the other hand, he who accepted the rigors of a discipline could submit himself completely to him. It is this unconditional obedience (from the latin "ob-audire", to listen) which is the true name of the love of the disciple for the master. Obedience is the core of all spiritual life, it alone can overcome the craftiness of our ego.

The exercises, always taken up again, cease to be painful and boring, for they become the very presence of the spirit of the master, to which one submits oneself in love. In other words, exercises are a relationship and that is precisely where all that we had acquired before the encounter with the master now enters into a new light. We can now practice the same exercises in a radically new way. This powerful presence of his person in every moment was meant to lead to a new stage, the most important one: the discovery of the inner Master. This is the purpose of true initiation. Instead of becoming attached to the master in an infantile dependency, Durckheim knew how to open the path toward the courage to be oneself and to listen to one's most secret core, there where the "still, small voice" can be heard calling us toward a completely personal development. Durckheim used no power over others, and his exceptional authority came entirely from his radiance. The master here gave way to the witness of a Reality which utterly surpassed him and which flooded his whole being.

This "Reality" could reveal itself, depending on the student, as Buddha, Allah, Krishna, or a cosmic Force. Durckheim loved you as you were and had such respect for the individual journey that he brought you to discover new depths in your own tradition. This love which was sufficient to itself and utterly free of proselytizing, was the greatest joy of the disicple. The greatest joy for Durckheim came when he felt in the disciple the same faith as his own, when he could bring the disciple into the depths of his own mystery whose radiance he named Jesus Christ. He could then share something of his personal substance and bring forth the secret of his life. For Durckheim, transformation is possible only at the core of our being. The radical modification of humanity and the future of the world depend on the spiritual experience. Human beings are sick in their very being. Wars and revolutions do not bring about fundamental changes. Durckheim "laid the axe to the root" (Luke 3:9) by choosing to deal with the genesis of human beings. We are at a turning point in history.

As in the Middle Ages, we must once again break through the fog of our degeneration. There will only be a new beginning through a return to the origin and essence of humanity, where a true rebirth can take place. In order to survive, humanity needs a spiritual revolution. It was the becoming of humanity which Durckheim dealt with and he therefore questioned all the institutions which pretend to care for it: the army, school, family, medicine, church and the kind of civilization they sustain. He presented a new way of living and being. All these institutions have much to learn from him, but it is especially the Church, which is meant to be an instrument for the fulfillment of humanity, which must hear his message. Durckheim is therefore infinitely more than a master who has come and gone. His voice remains that of a prophet among us, one of the pioneers of a return to the origins of Christianity. When he shows us how the East can reveal to the West its forgotten roots, this applies particularly to the Church whose roots are properly eastern. Meister Eckhart, Durckheim's great teacher, impregnated by the ancient Tradition, was a powerful revelation for him. His mysticism was a reaction to an invading rational theology which has never left us.

In communion with this master whose writings he never ceased to study, Durckheim broke through to the essence of the faith of the Fathers of earliest times: all his underlying metaphysical insight is trinitarian and he often said that nothing lives outside of the Trinity. This provides a fundamental vision of a human being who is both citizen of earth and of heaven. These two givens guide human destiny which is a path of transformation where the human being becomes God. Only this becoming justifies the presence of humanity on earth and every institution, especially the Church, which does not respond to the call inscribed in the heart of each being, betrays its mission. Durckheim believed that a God who becomes flesh and blood must be experienced! And every method: the Bible, the sacraments, our own body are first and foremost invitations to this foundational experience. The Church itself is nothing other than a place for rebirth. It is in this perspective that some disciples and friends of Durckheim join together in this book to express, each in his or her own way, how Durckheim made possible for them a new approach to Christianity. The purpose is not to praise a great master but to open the doors for which he gave us the keys and discover the new country which lies beyond them.

BECOMING REAL

14

THE LIFE AND WORK OF KARLFRIED GRAF DURCKHEIM

by Gerhard Wehr

At the dawn of the third millennium, we find a clear spiritual characteristic of our times: the traditional religious and ideological groups have lost their attraction. As with the authorities which made norms of them, the traditional dogmas and rules of behavior are being rejected and looked upon with skepticism. This is especially true of Christianity. There is much concern over the stagnation of ecclesial life and church attendance has been declining for a long time. The numbers of people leaving the Church is constantly multiplying. Paradoxically, in the face of this undeniable exodus, we witness a renewal of interest in spirituality. The word "spirituality" is used here to express the spiritual needs felt in our day and is therefore not to be confused with "religiosity" which refers to the structures of yesteryear. Against this background, we find the many propositions which were until recently considered marginal manifestations of the spiritual life. Their representatives were seen as elitists. If their tendency was religious, they were accused with disdain of being members of sects.

It is only when their search for an inner path corresponded with the needs of large numbers of persons that they have been looked upon in a better light. Among them is Karlfried Graf Durckheim. The spiritual practice which he presents is known under the name of "Initiation

Therapy." For several decades, Durckheim has been counted among those teachers of meditation and those therapists who have gained international importance. From his "Center of existential and psychological formation and encounter", founded in the early fifties with the psychologist Maria Hippius in the Black Forest, he has had a great impact in Europe. Durckheim's books were primarily based on his conferences and were widely disseminated. Countless seekers of truth, of all ages and social-economic levels, were attracted to him regardless of their ideological or religious affiliations.

Curiously, theologians and members of religious orders were constantly in his home in the village of Todtmoos-Rutte in the Black Forest to familiarize themselves with the practice of meditation. Many have testified having found with Graf Durckheim that which they lacked as Christians. It was no less than a rebirth of their spiritual life, even though -- or because -- Durckheim's "Initiation Therapy" did not focus on those goals. Rather, it dealt with the encounter between the person who is enclosed in his mundane self, his profane self, and his true Self. Durckheim speaks of a "Being beyond space and time." Seeking to introduce one to the experience of this dimension of reality, he explains: "To the traditional forms of therapy is added today a new one: a therapy of initiation. This is something entirely different. It deals with salvation. But the therapist is not the one who heals, that is, who intervenes with his own skills; he is a therapist in the original meaning of the word: a companion on the way. The word "Salvation" takes here its deeper meaning, its fundamentally religious meaning.

The aim is to pull man from his despair and lead him to wholeness. This despair is his constitutive condition: he is in despair because he is a prisoner of his I -- his Ego -- delivered over to the world, separated from his essential

Being, closed into his spatial- temporal condition, depending on his rational spirit and separated from Reality which transcends reason and whose nature is beyond time and space."

THE BEGINNING OF THE INNER PATH

Born in Munich in 1896 and deceased at Todtmoss-Rutte in 1988, Karlfried Graf Durckheim is the descendant of old Bavarian nobility. He grew up at Steingaden and at the Basenheim castle near Coblence where his parents had an important fortune before the economic collapse. A volunteer in the First World War, he renounced the property at Steingaden which was his as the first born. He studied philosophy and psychology. After his thesis, he accepted for a few years a professorship at Kiel. The officer on the Front, who did not hide his nationalism, could not have guessed that Hitler's coming to power in 1933 would mean the end of his professional career in higher education. Under the racist laws of national-socialism, he was thought to have "Jewish ties" on his mother's side. Yet he managed to be active in diplomacy and was for several years under the orders of the Reich's foreign ministry during the time of Joachim von Ribbentrop. It was in this context that Durckheim spent eight years in Japan, before and during the Second World War.

There he discovered the spirituality of the East, especially Zen Buddhism in its various expressions. It was only in the final years of his stay in Japan that Durckheim's life and ultimate work took on their particular orientation. And yet, this relatively late turning point, which occurred in his fiftieth year, had earlier origins. Already in his youth, the search for a way had manifested itself. As a twenty-three year old officer on his return from the Front after the First World War, he met his first wife Enja von Hattinberg. She introduced him by coincidence to the Tao-Teh-Ching of Lao-Tzu. There he read this verse of the eleventh aphorism: "Thirty spokes converge upon a single hub, it is on the hole in the center that the use of the cart hinges, we make a vessel from a lump of clay, it is the empty space within the vessel that makes it useful. We make the doors and windows for a room; but it is these empty spaces that make the room livable. Thus, while the tangible has advantages, it is the intangible that makes it useful." Durckheim described what occurred to him:

"And suddenly it happened! I was listening and lightning went through me. The veil was torn asunder, I was awake! I had just experienced "It." Everything existed and nothing existed. Another Reality had broken through this world. I myself existed and did not exist...I was seized, enchanted, someplace else and yet here, happy and deprived of feeling, far away and at the same time deeply rooted in things. The reality which surrounded me was suddenly shaped by two poles: one which was the immediately visible and the other an invisible which was the essence of that which I was seeing. I truly saw Being." We are therefore dealing with a Reality to which we can become transparent. In the history of philosophy we find many similar impressive testimonials from the experiences of Jacob Boehme (1575 - 1624) to Sri Aurobindo.

Despite differences in intensity, the common point in such experiences is found, as Durckheim suggested, in the fact that it cannot be confused with some uncontrolled feeling of well-being. This is not ecstasy or irrational divergence, but a grounding in the reality of the present. Yet the habitual universe of our mind has been broken through by the "beyond." How did Graf Durckheim integrate this experience? In what context did he place this tearing of the veil which separates, or seems to separate, sense perception from the supra-sensorial? In his essay on "The Practice of the Spiritual Experience," he tells us: "I had experienced that which is spoken of in all centuries: individuals, in whatever stage of their lives, have had an experience which struck them with the force of lightning and linked them once and for all to the circuits of True Life. They become conscious that it is not only a source of great joy, but also of suffering when this circuit is broken. At the same time, this experience reveals the unconditional mission which leads to the inner way."

THE PATH OF INITIATION

This mission has two sides: first, one must step onto this inner path; second, one is given the responsibility to help other persons who also seek this path. For a long time, the young man of twenty-three or twenty-four cannot begin this mission which consists of being the companion or "master" to others on the path. Even illumination does not dispense a solid formation. On the contrary, illumination requires a long process of maturation. It is a matter of initiation in which other stages of evolution must be undergone. But after this first experience, one is capable of deciphering the lived testimonials and the fruits of similar knowledge, discovering what they are in their essence and what they can be for a person who is beginning on the inner path.

On this subject, Durckheim stated: " "The attitude of conversion which gnawed at me from then on oriented me in a certain direction through everything I came across. It is not surprising that, in this context, Meister Eckhart created such an explosion within me. I could not put down his "Treaties and Sermons" which I perceived as an echo of the divine music I had just heard." It is precisely this music, even if its level and intensity were different, which he could perceive from that moment on in the writings of Rilke and of Nietzsche. Above all, it was the discovery of Buddhist texts which showed him the abundance, diversity and depth of similar experiences which persons on the way have left as a legacy over the centuries. In those remarkable "dialogues" with his friend, the French theologian Alphonse Goettmann, Durckheim explained how important Meister Eckhart had become for him. "I recognize in Eckhart my master, the master. But we can only approach him if we eliminate the conceptual consciousness."

Durckheim made it clear that he was not a specialist of Eckhart the "Magister" of scholastic philosophy who dealt in abstract thought. It was something else which attracted Durckheim: "There is such power in all that he says! That immense simplicity with which he speaks of God, the examples he gives, the problems he raises...There reigns in everything he says a certain atmosphere, the reality of the essential, the Real in the silence of the beyond, audible only to those who have ears to hear." Whoever speaks of the stages of an inner path must not give the impression that it is cut off from the world, as though we had to relinquish our obligations of daily life to lead the life of a hermit or of an ascetic.

This is not the case even when Durckheim uses a vocabulary that deals with initiation and mystery, exercise and transformation of being, or the experience of a numinous "beyond" which can suddenly seize us. He explains the "path" in this manner: "Beginning with an experience of Being, the Path progresses step by step at the heart of an initiation, of a knowledge and a melting down in which man comes out of the superficial existence of his ordinary consciousness and breaks through toward the depths of consciousness where essential Being can manifest itself in an active experience. At the threshold of this Path is an experience which signifies a conversion, a radical change of direction. From that moment on, a progressive metamorphosis leads man to Divine Being."

For Durckheim, it was the aphorism of the "Tao-Teh-Ching" which started his journey: "The experience of initiation is an overwhelming illumination which transforms everything. It is as though the thick fog breaks up and a new center is born, a new milieu and new meaning, the promise of fullness, order and wholeness." There are three factors which constitute the particulars of this path. In his book, "Hara", we read: "The first factor is the experience in which the light of Being shines in the darkness of existence. The second is the understanding of the relationship between the profane self and Being, recognizing the difference between the perception which falsifies the depth of Being and the true perception which opens us to life...The third factor is training, the exercise which destroys this false perception where the profane self is predominant and reconstructs the perception which is conformed to Being."

Seen in this light, the path toward this perception which creates itself little by little is a path of transformation of the whole person in his body-soul-spirit. One thing must occur for this to take place: training, whether in meditation or in exercises which integrate the body in this process of metamorphosis. This change which begins within does not in any way exclude the body. But before discussing this method, we must return to Durckheim's own search for the path.

IN JAPAN

Is it a search? Did the essential, the decisive, that which changed his life not occur by itself? Many events suggest this when we consider the critical years of the third decade of the twentieth century, during which time the professor from Kiel abandoned his activity at the faculty and accepted a diplomatic mission from the Brown Shirts in power. Certainly, a light had been lit within him years before when he heard the aphorism of the sage from ancient China. But the decision to launch himself into the spirituality of the East did not come at that moment. Other persons led him to it.

In his "Practice of the Inner Way", Durckheim wrote: "My sojourn in Japan is due to the fact that in 1936, having become "politically embarrassing", I was sent back to my post in the English section of the office of Ribbentrop and was flown to Asia on a scientific mission. The theme was: "Studies of the spiritual foundations of Japanese education." At that time, there was no question of an inner life for Durckheim. In the summer of 1938, the world political situation was tense. Hitler had just annexed Austria into the German empire. The fear of war was everywhere. It was then that Durckheim was sent on his special mission to Japan which would be of such vital importance to him. In the wave of enthusiastic nationalism, Durckheim saw himself as a useful representative of the "new Germany" for his people and his employers in Berlin, for the Minister of foreign affairs Von Ribbentrop, and for the Minister of education, Bernhard Rust.

The following is a passage from his diary dated June 7, 1938, the day of his first arrival in Japan: "At seven-thirty nine, the train leaves with the special wagon of the Norddeutschen Lloyd on the last stage of its journey across the continent. A magnificent sun, the furze in bloom, which has always been a good sign in my life. Thousands of thoughts and images cross my mind, both from the past and in imagination concerning the future. A representative of the N.D.I. appears and tells me that a large cabin is available for me. That is good to know." Durckheim is to voyage on the "Postdam." It will travel past Gibraltar and the Canal of Suez in the direction of Hong Kong and Shangai which is already under Japanese control. He arrives in Tokyo by mid-July. His colleagues await him. They are members of the national-socialist association of teachers and from the organization of the N.S.D.A.P.

No one asks him any questions; from the beginning, the conditions of his trip are clear. If it is true that the existence of a Jewish grandmother interferes with his professorial career at the university because of the infamous laws of Nuremberg, Durckheim gives no doubt of his loyalty to the National-socialist state. He authors a memoir in which he states the necessity of having an education specific to Germans overseas in the context of a general national-socialist teaching. He writes: "Based on my experience, I am certain that Germany, with the ensemble of its millions of citizens coming into contact with foreigners, possesses an instrument which can render immense service in the combat for its position in the world, if its contemporaries are uniformly educated for the particular responsibility which they encounter when dealing with foreigners."

These few assertions reveal the first motivations which guided Durckheim's two trips into Asia. And as his biography shows, it was not hard for him to obey the orders of his superiors. But in the background, there was always this other tendency toward the spirituality of the East, and especially toward Zen Buddhism; later it will be for Zen as a trans-religious attitude in universal man, the practice of spiritual exercise and disciplines. Graf Durckheim prepared himself in characteristic fashion when he wrote: "My familiarity with Meister Eckhart facilitated my approach to Zen. What does Zen teach? Every being in his original nature is a Buddha. His original face is disfigured by the mundane self. The condition of maturation whose fruit is a person liberated by his Buddha nature is therefore the death of the self and the experience of being." Even if Durckheim speaks in this context of the Buddha and the acquisition of the "Buddha nature," we must understand that what this ultimately means for him is not an introduction into Buddhist or eastern spirituality.

Rather he wanted to make accessible a specific experience generated by meditation exercises: "Exercise has a double purpose: to prepare the individual for the possibility of an experience of Being and for his metamorphosis into a witness of this experience awakening within. For illumination does not make an enlightened one! The more I penetrated into the experience and the wisdom of the exercise of Buddhism, the more it was clear that here was a universal understanding of the human being and his possibilities. This was a vision which, taking into account the liberation and salvation of man through health, efficiency and social fidelity, apprehended man in his deepest essence, whose experience and integration were also the conditions for the development of his true Self." From the outside, in the years 1930 to 1940, professor Karlfried Graf Durckheim seemed to be a cultural envoy of the Third Reich. At the same time, a subterranean process of transformation of which he was hardly conscious was taking place. "Out of personal preference, I came to know many Zen exercises. I even worked outside of meditation (za-zen), especially in archery and painting. It is surprising to notice that from the point of view of Zen, the most varied arts have the same purpose, whether it be archery or dance, song or karate, floral decoration or aikido, the tea ceremony or spear throwing...Done in the spirit of Zen, they are merely different ways aiming toward the same thing: the breakthrough toward the nature of Buddha, toward "Being."

One must master a technique, through much training, in such a way that, because we no longer need to do the work, an action from the depths comes into play and operates without the least intervention on our part." It was impossible to say where over the years this process of transformation would lead Durckheim. He traveled and lectured a great deal across many continents and in many cities. In his letters to his family in Germany, we find both his daily experiences and the discovery of spiritual teachings particular to each country. A note in his diary written in 1940 mentions the following: "We have a mistaken notion of Buddhism in Europe. It is seen as a passive doctrine which separates man from reality. Yesterday, I received a letter from my old friend in Kyoto, a priestess of Zen through whom I received my first initiation into the tea ceremony." He is in the midst of revising European prejudices which he and others hold in relation to Buddhism. Already, he is beginning a more intensive study of Zen Buddhism.

One day, he meets a young Japanese professor who speaks to him of his personal master with whom he is learning calligraphy and archery. The master would certainly take the German professor as a student. Durckheim accepts the offer as a sign of destiny. In his journal, we find a description of the first encounters with this Zen master: "I went to see the master at eight in the morning at his hotel. He is truly a fantastic person. There is something fabulous in these men! I stayed with him for two hours and the effect which emanated from him was such that in the evening I was still deeply affected..." He does not ask any questions for he is still under the charm of the exotic, personal impression of an extraordinary man. But if we follow Durckheim's notes, we will find a remarkable transition from his exterior responsibility as diplomatic official to a work on Being which occupies him more and more.

Certainly, he continues his professional obligations, but the freedom he is allowed in the organization of his workload makes it possible for him to combine his personal interests with his duties at the embassy. January 1941: Durckheim lives a whole year in Japan. He distinguishes three phases in his encounter with the Japanese spirit. The first phase deals with the ordinary Japanese; the second uncovers the traditional Japanese character expressed in Shinto, the cult of the emperor and the fulfilling of religious customs. But there exists a third phase which Durckheim describes at first only through allusions. In a letter to his family, he writes: "Third phase: there where a person realizes himself completely, discovering in his way the Divine. And that is of course what man feels most directly." Reflections such as these still do not reveal the distance which Durckheim is taking vis a vis national-socialism and his own concept of nationalist culture.

These two worlds still co- exist for him. He is attempting to harmonize his nationalist ideals and his spiritual interests. He does not yet realize that he will have to make a decision if he continues his inner path. He believes that what Zen Buddhism offers him is a gain to his exterior status. But on February 11, 1941, he makes the following remark: "In the meantime, I have enriched my life in an important way by beginning archery in my "big" space of two and a half meters."

ENCOUNTER WITH ZEN

Durckheim remembers having read an article by his colleague Eugen Herrigel dealing with the martial arts. He is therefore already familiar with the thought at the foundation of this special exercise which is Zen. And as his master of archery follows the same tradition as Herrigel, it is an added incentive to become initiated in this discipline. "That is what led me to begin this activity. I knew that I would learn things about Japan which would be useful to me and which cannot be found in books or in any other way." It seems that at this time he is still seeking information on Japanese Zen Buddhism. But he is learning that this kind of archery is not merely a sport, but a confrontation between the student and himself. That is the essence of the art, far beyond a simple technical skill. Whoever seeks only the latter misses the essential purpose which is an inner effort.

In his later letters, Durckheim states: "Archery gives a great tranquil force. Monday morning, the master was here and will return again tomorrow. Each time, we share long philosophical discussions on the problems of our times and on the essence of archery. Then we train for twenty minutes, shooting off six to eight arrows. It is a very strange thing, something entirely different than we might imagine in Germany. I will publish something on this subject some day." Durckheim kept his word, at least in that which concerns Zen in general. His master taught him that, for Zen, it is the same as for all serious spiritual effort: a certain exercise cannot be reduced to a sequence of life, whether it be archery or meditation.

Little by little, all the activities of life must be brought under the ordering power of the exercise. Daily life becomes the field of exercise. In his book "Daily life as Exercise," Durckheim expressed this discovery and this requirement: "Whatever we do, we do it in a certain posture. What we do is part of the world. It is how he does things that man manifests himself in his posture. This posture can be in accord with the inner law or in contradiction to it, permeable to essential being or inaccessible to it. For what is the right way to be here? It is that in which man is transparent to Being. To be transparent means to be capable of having the experience and revealing it to the world." If daily life, with its obligations and requirements, represents the field where that which is mastered in oneself must prove itself, we can then say that the inner way goes beyond simple interiority, for: "there where the inner work is successful, man can do nothing more than before, but he is different and he has become more: he has become another man.

Therefore, the visible work of the world is opposed to the man who is transformed internally. But these two things are intimately linked. The work of the world, which has real value, requires man's maturity, and his transformation leading to this maturity requires the suffering inherent in the creation of the work. Thus, inner effort and external work do not exclude each other but are indispensable one for the other. And as we are solicited from morning till night by both our inner being and by the world which is entrusted to us, the field of perpetual effort consists in reconciling these two aspects in daily life." It took nearly three years for Durckheim to learn to shoot an arrow without seeking to hit the target.

Forty years later, when he was eighty-seven years old, Durckheim did an interview on German television and spoke of that important moment: "I still remember the day, in the presence of the master, when I shot an arrow and it left on its own. "I" had not shot it. "It" had shot. The master saw this and took the bow in his hands, then took me in his arms (which is very rare in Japan!) and said: "That's it!" He then invited me to tea. That is how archery taught me so much, for the mastery of a traditional Japanese technique does not have as goal a performance, but on the contrary requires the achievement of a step forward on the inner path." Toward the end of his stay in Japan, Durckheim experienced the satori, the aim of Zen: a degree of illumination of reality. Through this he achieved the "spiritual break-through toward ultimate reality." In this way a greater Self is uncovered, beyond the ordinary self. This greater Self, and the destiny linked to it, does not spare a person on the inner way from trials. In the following stages of his life, Durckheim experienced an imprisonment of a year and a half in the prison of Sugamo in Tokyo under the control of the American occupation.

The letters maintained in his family archives are contradictory in nature: from moments of inner calm to profound depression. Decades later, in 1986, questioned by his biographer on his time in the Sugamo prison, he stated: "In spite of everything, it was a very fertile period for me. The first weeks I had a dream almost every night, some of which anticipated my future work. In my cell, I was surrounded by a profound silence. I could work on myself and that is when I began to write a novel. My neighbors simply waited for each day to pass. That time of captivity was precious to me because I could exercise zazen meditation and remain in immobility for hours." The years in Japan represent a special formation for Durckheim's later work as teacher of meditation and guide on the inner path. Yet his encounter with Zen and his study of eastern spirituality have created misunderstandings, as did his invitation to Buddhist monks and Japanese Zen masters to come to his center for initiation therapy at Todtmoss-Rutte.

He gave the impression, as professor, therapist and writer, of being one of the many persons who after the second world war transplanted to the West an Asian spirituality and way of life. In his works, Durckheim has always denounced these misunderstandings: "What I am doing is not the transmission of Zen Buddhism; on the contrary, that which I seek after is something universally human which comes from our origins and happens to be more emphasized in eastern practices than in the western. What interests us is not something uniquely oriental, but something universally human which the Orient has cultivated over the centuries and has never fully lost sight of." C. G. Jung, to whom Durckheim owes much in relation to depth psychology, pointed to the inevitable nature of the encounter between the East and the West, because it corresponds to the process of "individuation" (becoming oneself) of humanity.

BECOMING REAL

This encounter places an important responsibility on our cultures, now and for the future. But this is not a matter of imitating some exotic practice. At a conference which took place in Munich in 1930, Jung stated for example: "It is not with a simple sensation or a new excitation that we will help spiritualize Europe. Rather we should learn to acquire in order to possess. That which the East must give us is an aid for a work which we must do ourselves. What would be the use of the wisdom of the Upanishads or the revelations of the Chinese yogi if we abandoned our own foundations, as though they were past errors and, like pirates without a country, we would get hold of foreign practices?" That is why it is high time that the person educated in western style becomes conscious of his spiritual wandering and find his true self. Durckheim called that the "break-through of Being." It is a matter of accessing Being which is incarnated in each person in an individual way.

This is not mere speculation, nor the object of some faith however respectable, but the capacity of interiorization and an experience on the inner path. Would this possibility only have roots in the Far East because that is where Durckheim found it in such extraordinary fashion? In his conferences held in Frankfort, he stated: "I find it especially shameful that people say: the experiences of Being which Durckheim brings us are imported from the East. No, the experience of Being is everywhere in the world, even if it is given different names according to the religious life which has developed there, if we understand by the word "Being" the Divine Being. All reflection on Being begins with this experience...This experience can truly help man feel and assist him in living something contradictory to his usual self and his ordinary view of life, and make him suddenly experience another force, another order and another unity. It is obviously greater, more powerful, more profound, richer and vaster than anything else he can live through." In this way, Durckheim underscores once again that which links the hemispheres of the spirit and the aims of initiation therapy. East and West are then similar to the poles of a same reality which tolerates no division.

In this context, Jung spoke of the integration of the unconscious and of femininity into a whole which contains the image of the human being and of the world on the way to fulfillment. Taking hold of that thought, Durckheim made the following statement: "The earthly life of man is fulfilled in the realization of the totality of the human being, while emphasizing throughout history one or the other part. But this emphasis which is found in the East is an emphasis which each one of us carries more on one than on the other part. In each human being there is the feminine and the masculine. There is not simply a man or a woman but there is also the masculine in the woman and the feminine in the man. To be a whole man, one must therefore develop the feminine in oneself.

To be a whole woman, one must develop the masculine in oneself, without ceasing to be man or woman." And in order to invoke the need for the polarity of East and West, he added: "In the western spirit it is the masculine which dominates, and in the eastern spirit it is the feminine..." Already in his first book published on his return from Asia, "Japan and the Culture of Silence," Durckheim began to concern himself with this theme by interpreting what he called the "Eastern" has being the "counterpoint in the universality of our Becoming."

ON THE WAY TOWARD THE INNER CHRIST

To conclude, we must note another aspect which characterizes his becoming. This is the tendency (which slowly grew within him over the years) of aiming at a deeper understanding of Christ. In other words, Durckheim's spiritual path, toward which he was led and which he taught to others, is ultimately an inner path toward the Christ. "Next to the belief in a transcendent God there appears today the religion of an inner way founded on the experience of the divine which is developed through exercise and culminates in the metamorphosis which liberates man.

Next to a faith in liberation, which we can never provoke ourselves, is a conviction of a possible awakening to a divine Being living within us, in which we are "saved" from time immemorial, but from whom we have become separated by our human consciousness. But there is, as the West is beginning to recognize, the possibility of experiencing this methodically. This religion is nothing other than the manifestation of the inborn path toward our personhood, leading us through a rigorous discipline from the darkness of natural consciousness to awakening in the light of a superior consciousness." But we must not lose sight of two things: primitive Christianity already knew the inner path toward Christ.

The one who followed it had an inner experience. His whole life was a turning around, a "Metanoia." Whoever was transformed in this way saw themselves as a new creation. On this subject, the letters of the apostle Paul are among the primary documents of the New Testament, especially his letter to the Galatians. In other words, there always was an esoteric mystical Christianity of this type which could exist without an official representative of the Church. "The Spirit blows where it wills! Let no one slow it down!" He who is seized spiritually, the mature man, perceives the Spirit directly. Today, the numbers of persons led by their destinies toward this direct perception of the spirit are apparently multiplying. These are persons who have had particular experiences, "breakthroughs of Being" as Durckheim said. Independently from priests, preachers or "masters," they have perceived the call of the "inner master." In this way, a new experience of Christ can develop.

It is a matter of a "Being in Christ" which cannot or must not be replaced by the fact of being a member of the Church. Durckheim belongs, along with C.G. Jung, to those who have noticed this phenomenon from the point of view of the psychotherapist and have diagnosed it. In the fifties, he wrote: "We are finding ourselves today at the limit of the development of the western spirit which is characterized by repressing this vision and this experience, where natural consciousness opens to transcendence through supernatural experience. We speak here of the esoteric vision." This esotericism to which he refers is far from opposing to objective thought an interiority estranged from the world. Rather, it seeks to liberate the vision of a global dimension of reality. Spiritually related to Durckheim, the philosopher Jean Gebser spoke of "going beyond the mental conscience to the integral conscience."

This translates into a qualitative expansion of religious consciousness. Durckheim gives the ecclesiastical guardians of the faith something to think about: "The more the representatives of the faith focus exclusively on revelation and close themselves to the capacity of having an experience of the transcendent, the more they reinforce the position of the rationalists and of the unbelievers. That is where a transformation is occurring today. Neither the psychologists nor the psychotherapists of the past, nor the priests confined in their traditions can answer the impetuous demands which explode today from the despair of a youth alienated from the "faith," but thirsting for transcendence. Today, the transcendent reality penetrates with an irresistible force into the consciousness of humanity and wants to be seen both in living experience and in responsible action." Yet the specifically Christian element is still missing.

If we study Durckheim's work, it becomes clear that he slowly matured upon that path. His first books seem to avoid taking a religious position. Certainly they deal with a "call toward Being" or toward "the break-through of Being." But is this enough to be clear? The author suggests that whoever call upon his profession of faith or his inherited faith is not referring to a concrete experience. What happens then to the one who has no faith? Durckheim replies: "He has only the path of his own experience. This path can certainly be shown and consolidated by more experienced and advanced men in whom he trusts, but to find the path and to follow it belongs to each one in particular." This experience, however, and the path which corresponds to it, is beyond all confession. We cannot give it a religious label. "Yet we can call this great foundational experience a religious experience. Through it, a person experiences something which has a transcendental character.

We "taste" a numinous quality and are shaken by a power which raises us beyond our ordinary existence and links us to supernatural Being which is present within us." This being shaken is not only a powerful emotion which can accompany a spiritual experience. It is a characteristic of the path of initiation that the adversities of human life, aging, suffering, death -- in a word, the cross -- are consciously integrated. For, " the more a situation or a suffering seems unacceptable to ordinary man, the closer is the possibility of an experience of initiation, on the condition that he accepts the fundamental rule: to accept the unacceptable. We then have a chance to progress one step forward, to rise by one degree. It is in his attitude in relation to suffering, in his willingness to live it to the end for the purpose of liberating Being that man becomes the ally of divine Being."

One day, in the sixties, Durckheim no longer hesitated to accept this transcendent Being as a divine "You," but even entered into a personal relationship with it. He continued to use the same terminology, qualifying for example the path as "the path toward the Center." And the "inner master," as an urge leading and accompanying each person, received a name without confusion. When is man in his center? The answer is: "Man is in his center when he is one with Christ and lives through Christ in the world without ever leaving the voice of the inner master which is Christ and continually calls him toward the center. Here Christ is not only the "Being of all things," nor the intrinsic Path in each one of us, but also Transcendence itself...To the extent that man in the world is never entirely one with his being, it is only in the experience of encounter that this unity realizes itself. But in this encounter, if man experiences himself as person at the heart of the painful junction between heaven and earth, it is Christ who appears to him, not as a principle, but as a divine "You."

IN TOUCH WITH THE TRADITION OF THE CHURCH

Durckheim knew that he could encounter this divine "You" in worship and sacrament. These were not only stale teachings. It may be said that once his inner life opened onto the mystery of Christ, Durckheim felt the need to participate in the sacramental life of the Church. His disciples whom he had in the past introduced to Zen, as well as his closest colleagues, have not always understood this orientation of the old master who clearly had no particular interest in the institutional Church. It is important to note, however, to what extent Durckheim was close to the orthodox tradition. Various witnesses have testified to this, underscoring the attraction which he had for the piety of the Eastern Church.

Durckheim recognized that his spiritual source was Meister Eckhart, but also that at the center of his intimate meditative life was the "Prayer of Jesus" taken from the orthodox tradition and which is repeated as a mantra: "Lord Jesus Christ, Son of God, have mercy upon me, a sinner!" It is only through this concentration on the name of Jesus that all of Durckheim's other exercises coalesce. Once again, it seems that his intention was not to follow "eastern practices" in the West. Durckheim integrated it as a Christian, whether his adepts were aware of it or not. A man whose life is "under the sign of transformation" in the deepest sense of the word always remains on the path of a progressive becoming of the spirit, at the center of which lives the Christ.

It is therefore quite natural that he had an icon of Christ painted and always gave much importance to the celebration of the Eucharist, even during his retreat sessions. On his deathbed he called for an orthodox priest from Fribourg, Father Wolfgang Siegel. And Bishop Germain of the Orthodox Church of France hurried over from Paris to give Durckheim extreme unction several days before his death. But all this was possible and is justified only because its foundations were laid long ago. From that time on, Durckheim could witness to Christ as the "eternal Master," the one whom faith sometimes seizes, and who sometimes seizes us. And it is precisely in this context that we see to what extent he is linked to all those who, throughout history and in the present, enter this inner path, in the East as in the West, in the Christian tradition as in the tradition of other religions.

Durckheim referred to the "wisdom of early Christianity concerning religious experience." He added to that: "There is a difference between the pure mystic and the person on the path of initiation. The life of the mystic is a constant seizing by the Divine through transcendental experiences, while the person on the path of initiation works in an organized fashion toward the right attitude of the whole individual." Even if he gave great importance to experience, Durckheim energetically refused to make of it an absolute. Everything that has been inner experience must prove itself in life. Once more, then, the inner way and exterior work must correspond. Their reciprocal relationship is the same as that between the personal maturation of each person and the construction of the world and the responsibility toward all that exists.

From this comes a double duty: "The world requires of man that he impose himself by his efficiency, that he integrates himself and proves himself by his loyalty and his creative powers in the service of the community and of durable values. Yet Being present in our being requires that we oppose ourselves to the world and eventually stand over against the community...Rooting oneself in Being, contrary to appearances, is not contradictory to the requirements of the world: it is precisely the condition under which we can respond to them according to the criteria of Being. It is only through experience of Being within us that we can understand the world in its own being."

To enter upon an inner path as Durckheim did, as he taught and showed through his example, does not mean a retreat into an encapsulated Self. He left us with these words: "He who lives under the sign of the inner path attracts other persons seeking the path; for his way of reacting to all that happens, of placing himself at the level of some and not doing so for others, and his way of asking questions, involuntarily attracts the attention of the other upon that which is truly important to him and of which he suddenly becomes conscious. Soon, one will perceive himself in the wake of the other, and those who were first seekers of the path quickly become companions on this same path."

BECOMING REAL

DURCKHEIM THE THERAPIST

by Jean and Gisele Marchal

Even though he did not practice psychotherapy in the classical sense of the term, Durckheim has considerably expanded and transformed its use through his life and work. In its usual meaning, the goal of psychotherapy (whatever school or technique it may claim) is the healing and ameliorating of a neurosis which disturbs the behavior of the individual, interrupting his fulfillment and keeping him in a more or less permanent discomfort or even in depression and anguish. In this way of understanding psychotherapy, it is useless for the person who easily plays his social roles, who makes a living, maintains a stable family life, and lives his sexuality in a satisfactory way.

On the other hand, the person who is handicapped by some anguish (whether it be concerning death, illness, failure, or relations with the opposite sex), who goes from failure to failure in all his activities, who can only have conflicting and inharmonious relationships with his family and professional colleagues; in a word, who is constantly frustrated in his search for happiness, will need such psychotherapy which will be considered completed when his insertion into life will have become more equilibrated with less conflict and anguish.

For Durckheim, the concept of psychotherapy is entirely different: "Rather than eliminating troubles which have brought someone to Rutte, it is a matter of helping him take a step on the path of his self-realization." A person seemingly at ease in life, who achieves success, can remain in regards to the development of his inner being someone completely infantile who will remain frozen in this infantilism until his last breath without a particular work which would cause him to discover and integrate in himself his true dimension. The role of the psychotherapist in relation to such a person is then to help him or her become conscious of all the possibilities which lay dormant in a sort of fetal state, and to be a catalyst for the realization of the patient's potential.

"A distinction is being drawn between a small and large therapy. Small therapy refers to the treatment of neurosis and aims at mental health. Its goal is to make the subject capable of functioning in society. The first condition is to liberate him of his anguish, guilt, and isolation...It is a purely pragmatic therapy. But there are times when human suffering is rooted beyond that which can be accessed psychologically, reaching the core of our metaphysical being, located in the subconscious whose manifestations have a numinous character: the spiritual lie is then at issue. "Healing" is only capable if the person learns to perceive himself at that level. He must understand his failure in the world as the blockage of his self-realization through which his transcendent Being must break through. Such a therapy leads to a witness to essential Being in the profane self and, in that sense, to true Self-realization. That is large therapy. It must have a feeling of initiation."

THE ELABORATION OF PSYCHOLOGICAL
CONCEPTS

Early in his life, Durckheim developed a concept of human nature, its "essential Being" and its destiny. As a lieutenant in the German army during the four years of the war of 1914-1918, where he served on several fronts and most notably at Verdun, he was confronted with the fundamental experience of the three great trials which mark every human life: solitude, meaninglessness, and death. This discovery led him to leave the army and renounce his rights as heir to the family fortune. That is when he came upon Meister Eckhart and had the "great experience," the eruption of a new state of consciousness liberated from the limits of the ego.

Durckheim is led to the elaboration of a psychology and a psychotherapy founded essentially on the "call and the birth of a new consciousness." Such a consciousness is no longer imprisoned in the narrow limits of our "existential self" but points toward the liberation from the prison of the ego and toward the expansion into the limitless dimensions of "essential Being" through the development of a "cup consciousness" which directs the "arrow consciousness" as will later be seen. In 1923, Durckheim receives his doctorate in psychology and is married. He lives for a year at Kiel as assistant at the Institute of Psychology, then leaves for Italy to deepen his understanding of art, which is necessary for a "psychology of the whole person."

He returns to Germany and, in 1925, becomes assistant at the Institute of Psychology at Leipzig under the direction of Felix Krueger who originated the "gantzheit" psychology, "taking man as a whole and not as a sum of his faculties." In this period, Durckheim writes: "In my teaching, I sought less to communicate knowledge as to awaken students to inner experiences which seemed fundamental to me. Already at this time, the key to all science of man appeared to me as being the qualitative experience of his depths." Durckheim is then thirty years old; around the age of ninety, shortly before his death, when he still gathered about him small groups of disciples, his whole teaching was still centered on this "awakening to fundamental inner experiences." In 1931, Durckheim is named professor of psychology at the academy of Breslau.

Then in 1937, at the age of forty-two, he leaves for Japan, exiled by the Nazi government, where he will stay until the end of the war as attaché to the German embassy. Here he comes across the world of Zen. Master Suzuchi reveals to him the essence of eastern wisdom in a concise formulation: "Western knowledge looks outside, eastern wisdom looks within. But if you look within the way you look without, then you make of the within a without." And Durckheim wrote: "This statement reveals the whole drama of western psychology, which looks within in the way that we look at the outside world, making of it an exterior thing, that is to say, an object...and Life disappears!" In his teaching, Durckheim always insisted on the necessity in psychological work of going beyond this "objectifying consciousness" or "arrow consciousness" which makes of the inner world and object of study.

We must, on the contrary, enter into a "cup consciousness" made of openness and acceptance toward our existential reality here and now (just as the cup accepts the liquid which is poured into it, whether nectar or poison), so that it relies on this reality for the work of transmutation of the ego, and "makes of each situation, whether happy or miserable, agreeable or disagreeable, the best occasion to enter into the great experience."

Before his return to Germany, he is mistakenly imprisoned by the Americans for sixteen months. There he is again confronted with the experience of the absurd and of solitude, and he finds a "freedom absolutely independent of liberty as the world understands it," having the experience of true freedom within the walls of his cell, contrary to ordinary persons who feel free in the prison of the ego. Back in Europe, Durckheim creates in 1948 his center in Todtmoos-Rutte, near Fribourg-en-Brigsau in the Black Forest. He surrounds himself with colleagues trained in psychotherapeutic techniques developed by Madame Hippius (who will become the countess Durckheim). He receives there many seekers until his death on December 28, 1988, many seekers.

THE ORIGINALITY OF THE PSYCHOTHERAPEUTIC APPROACH

The great originality of psychotherapy according to Durckheim lies in two fundamental postulates. 1) The structure of the human being is Trinitarian: a person is not made of the conjunction between a body and a soul, according to the old but tenacious Cartesian schema, but is made of an essential reality, his "essential Being," through which he participates with the divine reality which is at the foundation of the universe, the Absolute through which the relative world exists. It is this divine reality, this Absolute, which animates the body and spirit through whose use the "existential self" enters into terrestrial existence.

In a normal life, it is legitimate to satisfy certain requirements of the "existential self" necessary for its harmonious and balanced development. But harmony and balance presuppose maturity and, once normal development has been attained, the "existential self" must be submitted to the true dimension of humanity and its true identity which is "essential Being": "The first reason for talking about a particular Dimension comes from the unique quality and imperious evidence of that which has been lived in the experience of "being touched by Being," and especially in the power of awakening to a new consciousness which fundamentally transforms us, making us free and responsible.

The experiences and encounters of Being call forth within us a new dimension of life and of consciousness which have remained hidden, that is, only secretly present." Durckheim insisted ceaselessly on this manifestation of essential Being hidden behind all visible reality: "From childhood, the hidden meaning of visible phenomena has marked my life. It constitutes an essential part of my therapy. Becoming conscious of Being hidden in all phenomena is linked to it. The words of Novalis: 'every visible is an invisible raised to the state of mystery,' has become of great importance for me with its implication of initiation. It deals with the awakening of the inner sense. He who perceives himself in his essential Being is also touched, through all appearances, by the Being of things."

2) To perceive oneself in one's essential Being is generally impossible for western persons without a particular prepatory work. The modern mind is clogged and unbalanced by all sorts of disturbing influences linked to education and a materialist environment, cutting off our spiritual potential and interfering with any normal integration. The suggestions of the media, which are becoming more and more powerful, multiply the false needs of the "little self" and enslave it to emotions and excitements which are increasing in crassness, establishing an almost insurmountable barrier between our ordinary consciousness and the consciousness of essential Being.

This is the worst form of neurosis in human beings at the end of the twentieth century, where even established religions are too often powerless to offer adequate remedies. "The development of modern society leads to a growing regression of individual creativity for the sake of impersonal collective realizations. Enterprise, the team, the State, the whole ensemble of bureaucracy, restrain the free blossoming of the creative individual. The imprisonment of these vital riches, through an invading rationalism, goes far beyond individual subordination necessary to the framework of society. We must attribute a good portion of the reigning uneasiness on modern civilization and the obstacles it places before the individual in his or her holistic fulfillment."

This growing unbalance created in the human psyche through the conditions of modern living explains the necessity for a specific work on the body and on the mind with the goal of leading them little by little toward emancipation from these problems which conceal our "essential Being" as thick clouds hide the sun and keep us from access to the pure consciousness of Being. "The resolution of neurotic troubles is, in most cases, the first condition for a contact with Being, and a cleansing of our inner terrain through depth psychology reveals the indispensable need for the therapy of initiation." Durckheim further points out that: "It is the contact with essential Being which liberates and facilitates the dissolution of the neurotic mechanisms of the self. It then becomes capable of renouncing its defenses when the center of man is found not in the self conditioned by the world, but in his essential Being."

THE THERAPY OF INITIATION

According to Durckheim, therapy is inspired by Jung's concept of the "Shadow" and of the work with the shadow as we will see further on. But before any theory, Durckheim insists on the importance of the quality of being of the therapist himself" "The influence of the therapist comes from the radiance of his being. The efficiency of his work only rarely originates from "analytical" theory and method, but always beyond the psychological, in the relation of a being with another being. That is where, touched in his ontological depth, the patient opens or closes himself up, enters the path toward healing or remains in his anguish." Jung also stated that psychotherapeutic work was not done "there" (pointing to the patient's forehead), nor "there" (pointing to his own forehead), but "there" (creating a great circle in the space between the two).

This is the "great Third One," who creates, sustains, inspires and animates the relationship between them. This "great Third One" is often expressed in the therapeutic relationship through significant events, completely inexplicable, which Jung called "phenomena of synchronicity" and which are one of the forms which the Absolute puts on to manifest Himself in the relative and to affirm in a striking way His Presence and All-powerfulness. For Durckheim, this therapeutic relationship relies on a specific work: work on the body, on the images and sounds which come from the patient (free drawing, clay-making, song, spontaneous use of a musical instrument, dance, etc.) which constitute the "exercises" on which is based inner development.

Durckheim insisted a great deal on the necessity of use of these exercises faithfully repeated each day in order to progress on the Way: "All training, understood as exercise, consists in a ceaseless repetition of the same action. During that time, the critical self as well as the will to competition, the desire to do through oneself, and self-love, must be eliminated." It is always a matter of a "disciplined service to oneself, leading to a way of being which allows the plenitude of Being to manifest itself."

But if the assiduously repeated exercise is necessary to progress on the Way, it is also true that all of life must become exercise: this is "daily life as exercise."

Durckheim tells us: "A Japanese friend asked me one day: When do you do your exercises? I answered him: one hour very early every morning. Then he told me: this shows that you have not yet understood anything. Either you do the exercise all day long, or you can do without it." If I had answered him: I exercise all day long, he would have said: you haven't understood anything yet, because without the particular exercise you will never make any progress in continual exercise." Here then are the particular exercises dealing with the body, the subconscious shadow (revealed through images), and continual exercise used in daily life.

1) Exercises for the body: These efforts deal with the body "that we are" as opposed to the body "that we have." Exercises dealing with the latter as they are practiced in the West always point toward performance, toward "having more." This is classic physical education as taught in schools, along with massages and other care of the body which is treated as an object whose performances must be enhanced or whose appearance must be embellished. These are the constraints imposed by modern medicine, which is exclusively in the service of the "body which we have" and loses sight of the interrelationship between organs, between the body and the psyche, and between the individual and the cosmos.

The "body which we are," on the contrary, is the body placed in service of the expression of our "essential Being," our original face, the immanent transcendence within us which is our ultimate reality. To put the body at the service of Being is to make it "transparent to transcendence." The exercises for the "body which we are" seek to make us conscious of right attitude, right gesture, right tension, right breathing. Right attitude is centered in the hara, which "defines the foundation of man. Hara represents the vital center of man, the earth center. To be rooted in this center is to be open to the powers of renewal of the cosmic life." This attitude, realized in a perfect way in the posture of the Buddha in meditation, is nearly the opposite to that of the Greek disc-thrower focused toward a goal and a performance (to throw the disk as far as possible), has unbalanced in space as the Buddha is stable and deeply rooted.

The attitude of the disc-thrower perfectly symbolizes this "arrow consciousness" always aiming toward a goal and which makes of the body the instrument of this will to power. The search for the right attitude, animated by the hara, presupposes the "right tension" and the "right gesture": "These are the gestures through which man presents himself, the signs of his Being." Finally, in right breathing, we are breathed in by the great Life which expresses itself through the "body that we are": it breathes through us. "Breathing represents the movement of the Creative Life which, in each moment, dissolves that which threatens to harden us, in order to give birth to a new form. Work on breathing represents a transformation of the whole man. One must understand that superficial breathing is an expression of the man who keeps himself from becoming a Person. The self blocks the path toward transcendence."

The therapeutic use of these exercises dealing with the "body that we are" is one of the most original and precious aspects of the psychotherapy developed by Durckheim. It is impossible to speak of this therapy without referring to these corporal exercises which represent a heresy to the adherents of classical psychoanalysis. There is also another heresy: at the end of his life, Durckheim insisted on the importance for the therapist to establish at certain moments during the therapy a physical contact with the patient, and he would tell the therapists whom he advised: "Touch them!" Just as the great Third One animates the relationship of "soul to soul," He also animates the contact of "the body that I am and the body which you are."

2) Exercises for the "Shadow" Here, the subconscious must always be left to express itself through spontaneous creativity. "Meditative drawing," modeling with clay, free use of a musical instrument without technical training, dance, song. Especially in free drawing or work with clay, the repressed contents within the "Shadow" can take shape and allow one to become conscious of the sleeping dynamism which they reveal. The shadow "represents the whole of our unlived vital functions which have been repressed...There are tears which we have never shed, laughter which we have never let out, aggressions which we have not dared to release. There are original impulses which were not allowed to us." In Durckheim's therapy, the aim is to "become a person" in the etymological sense of the word (per-sonare): becoming transparent to the Transcendence which is within us. This is a work of transformation and maturation. The very obstacles on the path of transformation will make it possible for us to progress. When left unrecognized or when they are not overcome, these obstacles constitute our shadow.

"On the inner path, it is not possible to jump over our shadow. We must recognize this repressed life, accept it and integrate it." Durckheim adds elsewhere: "Only the person who accepts the darkness within himself and around him, and who does not shrink from it when he encounters it in new ways, can manifest Being in the world. For Durckheim, the shadow clothes itself in different aspects of which he distinguishes three kinds. First the repressed expressions: "Those which could have been part of our true being, but which we have not admitted...It is always a matter of an inner tension which we do not let out." This tension, which is not allowed expression, often becomes a source of de-pression. The second kind of form is the one which results in unaccepted invitations: "You walk by a bakery and are tempted but do not enter!" The third kind of shadow rises from our imprisoned essential Being: "In the shadow is also imprisoned our true nature, our inner Christ, our essential Being...Repressed Being is prisoner of our existential being.

Each experience in which essential Being is liberated for a brief moment should be accompanied by becoming conscious of that which blocks the path toward Being." And Durckheim also states: "The refusal in our consciousness of essential Being produces the deepest shadow. This shadow is, however, repressed primordial light." This third kind of shadow shows us that it is not only constituted of negative elements, nor uniquely made up of all the things we refuse, repress, and hide to others and to ourselves. The shadow also carries positive aspects, among which is the feminine dimension ("anima"), unknown to man and often also to woman. These are qualities which have not yet been consciously developed. For Jung, who inspired Durckheim, the shadow is completely unknown to the clear and conscious self. Durkcheim writes that "the shadow is the light in the form of that which hides it." This statement expresses the fact that, by working with our shadow, we can liberate this light which is in our depths.

Durckheim insists on the fact that one of the roots of this shadow goes back to childhood: "The repression of the vital impulses of the child, caused by discouraging words, a lack of understanding and love, impedes his natural impetus. It stops him from becoming conscious of his supernatural essence and from developing it...We must become conscious of the discomfort of our repressed essential Being, then eliminate it through appropriate means." These appropriate means for work on the shadow are especially: --directed drawing (our meditative drawing) developed by Maria Hippius --clay sculpture --work with the voice and with musical instruments Meditative drawing is practiced with eyes closed in order to facilitates the spontaneous arising of images from our subconscious expressing aspects of our shadow, particularly those repressed and unexpressed creative forces. With clay sculpture, we let our hands freely manipulate the earth.

Forms then appear which also reveal repressed energies or archetypal figures which can "make our metaphysical Being resonate." These two modes of expression allow us to create a visual representation of the contents of our subconscious which makes possible discoveries which can be surprising and frightening, but always necessary: "It is important that each woman recognizes the witch within her, and that each man recognizes the wolf within him." It will then become possible to dialogue with these aspects of the shadow which have thus been revealed. We also find a double aspect in our work on the voice: on one hand, we become conscious of the "level on which we are speaking" and of the blockage of this expression (a timid voice, one that is too weak or too shrill, etc.). These exercises also teach us to progressively modify such defects of expression: "Learning to observe one's voice is to perceive within it one's inner master."

The work with a musical instrument is done with pure sound, "as a mirror of one's own purity or impurity." The level of the patient's presence will be revealed according to the improvised rhythm. Finally, a mode of expression also counseled by Durkcheim is found in writing: "The path toward liberation will take several varied forms: for example, to put to paper some situation of conflict which has remained unattended and which oppresses the heart; to be able, without any constraints, to transcribe that which overwhelms us with guilt, fills us with anger or makes us look back on the past in despair. To express everything through writing with absolute sincerity can bring great relief, a real liberation leading toward a new stage of evolution. It is often unnecessary that a third of it be read, it must only be written: all one's furor directed against someone in a definitive letter!" 3) Spiritual exercises in the therapy of initiation Independently from these repeated exercises dealing with the body or the psyche, Durckheim greatly insisted on the importance of spiritual work which constituted meditation in zazen posture.

In this meditation, one must dive into the great silence beyond the mind, letting the wave of the ego rejoin its essential reality which is the ocean of the pure consciousness of being, expanding the limits of individual form to the limitless dimensions of the essence of all form. Meditation brings forth the mysterious feeling of participating in a cosmic body which embraces and immensely surpasses the limits of our own body: "The meditator feels himself, in this belonging, both protected and in contact with the universe from all sides. The Peace which invades him then engenders a disposition of spirit which exterior noises cannot trouble. If the meditator is well trained, this inner disposition stays with him when he comes out of immobility and begins moving about." With the exercises dealing with the discovery of the "body that we are" and those leading to the expression of the shadow, we are working toward the patient search for our essential Being. Through meditation, we no longer seek anything, but attempt to be found by Being. Durckheim often said: "You do not have to seek, but to let yourself be found by the transcendence within you."

The condition to let oneself be filled is to be empty. "So that the break-through toward the plenitude of Being may occur, the multiple must disappear. But the emptiness suggested here is more than the absence of the multiple. It is charged with an annunciating quality of mystery, the mystery whose access is through the faithfulness of the path of initiation." Durckheim added: "Creating emptiness in oneself is also for the Christian a first condition for an authentic "Christian" perception of existence...One must open the eyes and ears of essential Being so that the blind may see and the deaf hear...To accomplish this, one must first free oneself from images, especially those which represent God. It is therefore the realization of this emptiness which make possible in the meditator the sense of the fullness of Being." 4) Daily life as exercise Along with these particular exercises, regularly repeated, based on the body and the expression of the shadow or on an entrance into the depths through zazen, there is for Durckheim an even more fundamental exercise which is practiced all day long: it is called "daily life as exercise."

This is a matter of living every circumstance, whether joyful or distressing, in which existence inserts us day after day, without being pulled out of our center by emotion, refusal or repulsion. This presupposes the necessity of "accepting the unacceptable." According to Durckheim, the unacceptable, with which every individual is eventually confronted, holds three particular aspects: annihilation, the absurd (or meaninglessness), and solitude. "There are three fundamental distresses in the human being: the fear of annihilation, despair before the absurd, and infinite sadness in the face of solitude. Death, meaninglessness and solitude are and remain the enemies of the natural self...The transcendent dimension of life can suddenly appear in these boundary situations. But this can only happen if man realizes this paradoxical exploit which the ordinary self could never achieve: to consciously accept to undergo the dangerous experience of auto-annihilation." Durckheim evokes the certainty of inevitable death (under bombings for instance) where, suddenly, it is given to persons to "consciously abandon themselves to the inevitable.

The unbelievable can then occur...There is an absolute calm, an indefinable feeling of happiness. Another life has touched them. This same experience can be felt by those who are fatally ill. " Similarly, before a senseless, absurd, incomprehensible situation (such as betrayal by the beloved), "if he is capable of accepting the unacceptable, he can suddenly have access to a feeling which goes beyond the meaning and meaninglessness of this world, just as the preceding dealt with the sense of a Life beyond life and death." Finally, when a person accepts complete solitude: "He can then experience an inconceivable protection, even though he is abandoned by the world. In these three cases, the acceptance of the unacceptable is neither heroism nor resignation, but the experience of an unknown freedom through which he transcends his habitual self. At the heart of annihilation, of the darkness and cruelty of this world, man has access to a Power, a Clarity, and a Love which can be described as "superhuman" because he experiences them in contrast to the requirements of the world!

During such an experience, one can distinguish the three-fold structure of supernatural Being: Being as creative Fullness, foundational Law of meaning and order, and integral Unity." 5) Taking seriously the moments when we experience the "Touch of Being" In the years 1970 to 1980, and right to the moment when illness forced him to renounce it, Durckheim gathered around him every year at Rutte a little group of some twenty French persons. For a whole week, we gathered around him after the sunrise meditation in the kendo. During these meetings, each of us was invited to share one of those moments when we were "touched by Being" or "moments lived in the presence of the sacred." It did not necessarily involve the imminence of death, the absurd, or solitude, but the sudden experience of an infinite Reality which erupted in our life beyond all rational explanation and which, for that reason, we have a tendency to relativize, forget or neglect.

Durckheim would comment on each of these experiences, pulling out of every story "the quality of the contents of the experience," and insisted on the necessity for taking seriously these "touches of Being" and the numinous which they revealed. We would then recognize in those moments the eruption of a manifestation of the infinite and absolute Reality in our little relative world, briefly exploding our usual views and assumptions. During these meetings, it was clear that each person had witnessed one or more of these "privilege moments" during the course of their lives. Such experiences are much more frequent than we realize, as we often do not recognize their "numinous" character. Durckheim was in the habit of saying that there were four privileged areas in which one could experience the numinous: contemplation of nature, encounter with another person in an erotic exchange, authentic art, and religious worship.

These are always moments which are out of the ordinary when "you are touched by a immense Reality which suddenly places you in a state of security, consolation, and especially profound joy which you do not know in your existential life...These initiating experiences always create the birth of a new consciousness where a little voice says: "Listen. You have just had the experience of something extraordinary; it must become more than a nice memory; it is something which shows you your deepest core. Get upon the path, accept the exercise of a discipline and try to transform yourself in such a way that you, as an existential being, are capable of witnessing in daily life to this deep reality." If man accepts this counsel, he progressively becomes from that moment on the witness of the divine reality in everyday life." To accept the idea of a discipline and to regularly practice an "exercise of initiation" is therefore an integral part of taking seriously this experience. That is why, every afternoon at Rutte was devoted to the exercise of one of these disciplines for confronting the subconscious. The goal, and sometimes the result of this "therapy" according to Durckheim, is to reach the "quality of the numinous" (Jung, R. Otto) in which is revealed the transcendent Reality which exceeds the limits of the natural personality. When this transcendent Reality becomes definitively the center of life, man has reached the highest stage of his development: he has truly become a "Person."

This implies a release from the pretension of the natural, rational, moral order of the personality and the entrance into a new freedom and to a new responsibility. This experience of the "breakthrough of Being" has always been the decisive event in the life of human beings toward their full maturity." As Durckheim often stated, it is a matter of becoming "transparent to the immanent transcendence within," in such a way that "we are definitively rooted in another depth." This is the "therapy of initiation" developed by Karlfried Graf Durckheim. "It accompanies man on the Way which is truly our life and our truth. It is the path toward a disposition which makes us always more permeable to that Being which has surfaced within through the experiences of its "Touch." This Being present in our being seeks to manifest itself in the world. To make progress means to become such that we are capable of translating these experiences through the radiance of our way of life, through the witness of a luminous presence, and through our way of thinking, acting and loving in the world."

INCARNATION: THE BODY OF OUR CONVERSION

by Bernard Rerolle

Consciously and unconsciously, did not the teaching of Karlfried Graf Durckheim on the body nourish itself on the Christian tradition? And can the teaching of Christian spirituality revitalize itself through a contact with Graf Durckheim? Do not both of them have as center the mystery of the incarnation? For many decades, the Christian West has lost sight of the role of our body in the exercises of our spiritual life. A powerful current of thought has treated "brother donkey" as a trivial and despicable instrument, even though it was given to us from the beginning "in the image of God" to serve in the process of our transformation into beings of light. And there has never lacked missionaries to export this bastardized spirituality to the four corners of the earth.

But times are changing and the old inhibitions are being pushed aside more and more every day. Is this good? Is this bad? It is certainly not without resistance that they respond before the aggressions of our societies and our cultures, before the permissiveness of our images and of our ways. But for those who can read the signs of the times, it is clear that inhibitions are being unbound, as were unbound the wrappings around the corpse of Lazarus, and spiritual life enters into its own thanks to therapies, martial arts, dance, corporal expressions, gestures of prayer and of liturgy.

"TO HAVE A BODY" IN ORDER TO GO SOMEWHERE

At Rutte, the suggested exercises deal with our body but we quickly understand that they deal ultimately with spirituality. And we also quickly understand that this work is inscribed in the straight line stretching from the most ancient and venerable traditions of the East and of the West. This work relates to their finest epochs of fervor and balance, and to their greatest sages. Karlfried Graf Durckheim is also one of those who saw clearly through the modern chaos of all that deals with the body, in the countless currents of psychotherapy, etc. While the elements of wisdom which we need are quite often buried in techniques, fashions, approximations, he has been able to extract and re-orient them. Durckheim always resisted being considered a theologian and kept his distances from doctrines and hierarchical structures of organized religion. But the respectful interest which he held toward the Gospel only grew over the years as more theologians came to consult with him for their own existence.

He tirelessly underscored our condition as unfinished beings, incomplete, pulled between heaven and earth; he reminds us of the crack which exists between "the body that we have" and "the body that we are." It is unfortunate that we only have one word to describe the body which we train for sport and show to the doctor and the one through which we express our personality, our tenderness, or our faith. As much as "the body that we have" is easy to see, so is it difficult to accept when we become handicapped or separated from it. This body imposes itself on us physically, psychologically, economically, socially...and it is necessary that we take it into consideration with all the attention it deserves and that we organize its toiletry, its nutrition, its work, its healing. All these cares are the first stage, the obligatory basis of the spiritual; it is therefore necessary to integrate the sciences and techniques which the modern world puts at our disposal.

It is in relying on the work of psychologists that Durckheim leads us to observe the quality of this first stage. The quality of our rigidity or our suppleness, of our breathing or our attitudes and gestures are symptoms of that which hides from our consciousness, in other words it is our "shadow." This shadow creates the obstacles which keep us from going where we wish to go. To diagnose this shadow from the symptoms which express themselves corporally will require patient, precise, lucid attention, without complacency. And for this work we will need the help of a competent therapist who opens our eyes: he will teach us to make this "body that we have" play its role as instrument of auto-analysis and auto-healing. It will be the humble gestures of daily life lived with love and attention which will be the field of battle as we "seek the Kingdom." This first stage already brings us closer to the Gospel.

There is life only in the evolutionary process inscribed in the body of an individual and in the duration of his existence. This evolution never regresses, but leads somewhere. Where does it lead? Toward some finality for individuals and for the human species? We cannot answer this question at this first stage, but we are able to recognize that our situation is strange, inexplicable: whether we want it or not, through our birth in a body, we are thrown on an evolutionary trajectory or, as Carl Jung would have it, on a process of individuation. Everything occurs as though we had received our body so that we might go somewhere. Jesus brought healing of the body to certain handicapped persons. The goal of this work was not to do a theological demonstration, by using these men and women as instruments. Nor was it that Jesus was moved by certain individual distresses in an ocean of pain. It would be better to say that Jesus wished to help these people in taking up their journey toward someplace else, because this someplace else was hidden to them by their infirmity. No one will ever exhaust all the meanings of these miracles.

Notice the importance which Jesus brought to the body that we have: the importance of healing, of shared meals and of caressed children; the importance of Mary Magdalene's perfume and of the grilled fish on the beach of the Resurrection...It is astonishing to think that in certain recent times, the meaning of the body was so lost by believers that they pushed aside the miracles as disturbing and useless passages of the Gospel! (Truly, the human mind is capable of everything!) At the center of the mystery of Jesus, there is the Mystery of his Incarnation, and this is a mystery which he shares with us. It is intentionally that we do not deal here with the mysterious gesture with which Jesus broke bread and said: "Take and eat, this is my body!" This would take us beyond the limits of our subject.

"TO BE A BODY," THE MYSTERY OF
INCARNATION

Durckheim invites us to rely on the perception of the body which we have in order to enter into the perception of the body "that we are," the one which never lets itself be seen spontaneously, however paradoxical that may seem. Our gaze must accept to be released from the anxieties which cloud it: the need to understand, to objectify, to dominate, the weight of our past and the need to justify ourselves...We must let a new gaze be gently born within us, a creative and poetic gaze, the gaze of a believer. This is a gaze capable of situating the things of our life, however small or banal they may be, in the vast perspective of their infinite meaning. This is the gaze of a prophet (the man with the penetrating gaze), who knows not to stop at appearances and words and truly sees events for what they are. To perceive the body that we are is to go beyond the land of ideas to enter into the one of concrete reality.

"That which our hands have touched, and our eyes seen of the Word of Life," said saint John. In the expression "body that we are", it is the verb "to be" which plays the pivotal role and helps us to balance the word "body" in a new meaning, allowing us to see ourselves with a gaze renewed by poetry. Durckheim often emphasized that there is a great difference between "being" and "living". To say that we "exist" is to say that we are entirely submitted to space and time, that we are completely circumscribed in the limits of our skin and of our individual history, that we are defined by our professional and social roles or by the circle of our relationships. Our life, as "existence", lets our transcendental dimension appear only with great difficulty. Yet many human beings limit their horizon to their existence: to work, to amass, to enjoy, to wait, to submit...

To the extent that they refuse to break out of this closed horizon, we can say that they "exist" but "are" not. To say that "we are" is to move onto another plane, a mysterious one, halfway between space-time and the beyond. It is the level of mystery on the way to realization: the mystery of our incarnation. At the time of our adolescence, for example, at the time when our personality moves out of the matrix of our childhood, at the time when our concern for hairstyle and toiletry arise, our behavior of seduction and rejection, etc., we begin to perceive within us a being still unknown who seeks to express himself in our body: to "incarnate" himself. And this overwhelms us, it is the famous crisis of adolescence. One of the first steps in the long series of crises which mark our journey toward somewhere else. The very first of these crises is none other than the moment of our entry into the world and of our first "breath" (unless it was preceded or prepared by some crisis "in utero").

This process of crises is completely inseparable from our life, it manifests itself from our first moments and will not let us go until our last breath: and if it is at the center, it is because it is a manifestation of the mystery of incarnation. The word "incarnation" does not describe the fact that we have become several pounds of flesh and bones, but the fact that through our face, our attitudes and gestures (and even through our clothing and our familiar objects), "something express itself", an invisible makes itself visible. Durckheim loved to quote the poet Novalis: "The visible is an invisible raised to the state of mystery." Can we go further? What is it exactly which incarnates itself? The gaze of the poet and of the believer is necessary to perceive a little light in this direction. That which incarnates itself is not only the half-mystery of our conscious and subconscious psychology, but a dimension of our being vertiginously deeper and ineffable: the Mystery of Spirit, the Divine Spark, the "Imago Dei." Because they lived daily life with Jesus ("We who have eaten and drunken with Him"), the disciples began to doubt the presence of mystery.

And suddenly, in the period of crisis (once again!), Jesus asked them: "Who do you say that I am?" The disciples understood perfectly that He was not asking them: "How do you like the way I live?" But they also felt that they had no words to answer that question. Their response expressed only a little bit of the reality, but left out the field of infinity: "You are the Messiah..." This being which seeks to make itself known through our flesh manifests itself, for example, in our need to be someone and to be loved. Or more exactly, in the power of that need: it is so extraordinary that we become seriously ill if we cannot honor it or if we simply let it be perturbed. Such a power is clearly the sign that this being comes from far beyond us. The question "Who do you say that I am?" is asked as soon as two human beings meet one another. If they stop at their existential dimension, their dramatically short sight will only offer them an existential reply; but it is a great temptation to remain there since we do not have at our disposal the words to respond, to say to the other: "You are God," even if we loved them a great deal.

Whatever our social, professional, or religious situation, our behavior, our language, our clothing will speak first of our existence and little or not at all of our being. Why does the latter hide himself so carefully? This produces in us more than mere perplexity, but anguish. When we seek to know who we are or who the individual is whom we are dealing with, our gaze falls upon this defense as on a wall of darkness and impenetrability. Those who have stopped loving themselves (or never knew how) will quickly reject banging their head on this wall. They will satisfy themselves with certain cheap explanations such as: this being does not exist, or if he exists, he has no importance or he is too fragile and should not be touched, or he is a terrifying monster which must never be disturbed...

Only if they become poets and/or believers, if they become lucid through love, can their gaze pierce through this strange wall. Most often, it is the loving look of our neighbor who breaks through and lets in the light. This is the case with awakening love, needless to say, but also with the encounter of a "therapist" through whom the current can pass. We cannot help but think of the gaze of Jesus when he said: "Rise and walk!" to a paralyzed person; or when he said: "Go, your sins are forgiven!" to some man or woman disfigured by a disordered existence; or when he said: "Your faith has saved you!" in healing some infirmity...In these situations, Jesus showed himself poet and creator in corporal reality. The verb "poiein" (from which our word "poet" comes) means "to do, to create". Jesus made himself fully present and available to this being, this spirit which lived in his body and wanted to express himself, to speak. In Hebrew, da-bar which means word, also means event: Jesus did not speak to offer ideas but to create events.

We must not conclude from this that he was a being set apart, having nothing in common with us. On the contrary, being a poet, he revealed to us that this same being, this same spirit, is hidden in the depths of "every man coming into the world", that it is at work behind each of our walls, seeking to express itself, to speak, to create an event. Jesus never ceased to make us conscious of this in every possible way. And if he went as far as to give his life for those he loved, it was for the purpose of their realizing what is at stake. Many, under his gaze, have felt themselves reborn, have risen up to undertake a new life, or at least a new stage in their lives. Having believed in their being from the word of Jesus, they have taken up again the process of the mystery of the Incarnation in their body. And this process did not isolate them in a little, self-involved work on themselves. Like all blossoming of life, this discovery has contained within it a dynamism which called upon them to share.

These persons have made it their duty to transmit the good news through their witness, their care of the sick, the sharing of their goods and through all sorts of signs and wonders. And this has been going on for two thousand years. This is clearly a sign that Jesus does not have a monopoly over the poet's gaze. Christians are not the only caretakers of this wealth. The presence of being and the capacity to break through the walls of the ego is known in all places and throughout time, put into practice by the great religions of the world. The mystery of the Incarnation must be at work in every human being. John called it "the light which came into the world for every man." It is therefore not an artificial bridge which Durckheim sought to re-establish between all persons of good will. The therapies at Rutte fit perfectly in this great universal legacy. For more than thirty years, Durckheim and his colleagues have pronounced innumerable times: "Rise and walk!" They do it as men and women of good will, with the means which are available to them. They do not remain on the level of moralizing exhortations but put in action corporal processes.

They specify that they do not close themselves into the domain of purely medical efficiency, but leave open the doors to the beyond. To those who come to them to find release from crisis, they announce that the time of their crisis is precisely the time of their opportunity. And they undertake in space and time certain exercises which only find their full efficacy and meaning if they are done in the context of that which is beyond space and time. At the beginning of morning meditation, one of Durckheim's exhortations had as theme the sign of the cross: the universal symbol of two dimensions which cross each other in us, the here and now and the beyond.

INCARNATION AS PROCESS AND PURPOSE OF EXERCISE

From crisis to crisis, each of us reaches maturity (as best we can) with unequal opportunities according to our physical, psychological, emotional, intellectual, social and spiritual potential. Progress occurs through the linking of events which usually unfold in a certain order and presuppose the generation of all sorts of energies. This process of individuation takes time and occurs according to two complementary movements: the movement through which our consciousness is awakened through maturation and the movement through which our consciousness favorizes our maturation. These two movements take time and require untiring exercises from us. Filled with dreams and contradictory desires, we move through life unsteadily, in a body which is unbalanced, rigid and awkward. Moreover, we let ourselves be rocked to sleep by so many entities: the couple, the family, the profession, the group, fame, routine, and even religion in certain cases! Yet, our path may sometimes cross by chance that of a Master, or perhaps that of one of his disciples, or we may simply meet someone whom he has healed.

This is an opportunity, particularly if we experience this encounter as an invitation to change, to evolve, to be transformed, to be converted, to enter upon the path of inner practice. We are invited to begin from the "body that we have", such as it is, listening to what it tells us. We are invited to launch out on the discovery of the "body that we are", which is nothing less than to participate in the mystery of our incarnation. It is a long journey, full of ambushes from outside and from within and our imagination quite often amplifies these obstacles to transform them into nightmares and make them insurmountable. The help of the Master and of his companions is indispensable to guide us in this maze: they lead us to the threshold of the mystery which we are and this is our initiation. One of the first ambushes, which is most fearsome to westerners in the twentieth century, would be to confide the reins of our evolution to our mind and to let our efforts wander far from the real.

Those who are passionate for conferences on this subject and then return to their daily life without changing anything resemble the man of whom saint Paul said that he looked into a mirror and then forgets immediately who he is. For them, inner practice becomes an absolute necessity. The believers say in their Credo: "The Word came down from heaven and became flesh..." Do they always sense to what extent these words express the depth of their condition as human beings? What is more important for them than to let their being become flesh as did the One whom they consider "the first among many brethren"? Perhaps they add too quickly: "And he returned to the heavens"? Is it not because the process of the incarnation of being is common to all persons that we share it with the Christ? To hold this reality at a distance from our concrete life, under pretext that it is a mystery, is to commit a major, irreparable error. Jesus was not an extra-terrestrial from another world.

The Scriptures tell us that it was because he was "pressed by the Spirit" that he went into the desert, that he asked John to baptize him, that he begins to preach, that he went to Jerusalem. Yet it is his own spirit that is referred to and this spirit made him realize his incarnation on a progressive rhythm, as our spirit does for us. "He shared in all things our human condition". His body became more and more transparent to the divine light, and while he agonized on the Cross, a witness cried out: "Truly, this man was the Son of God!" For three years Jesus did his inner practice to respect the rhythms of human life. He needed time for that. Otherwise we would not be able to keep from thinking that his whole adventure was only a scenario to get around the limits of our liberty! The stages of the life of Christ can serve as landmarks and invitation to our own journey. Born in a body, it is as a body animated by the Spirit that we advance from event to event, from crisis to crisis.

If Jesus said so often "Rise and walk!" was it not because he first put it into practice himself? And do we not hear this injunction in the depths of our being? Do we not also hear the "Come and follow me!" so often imperceptible? Durckheim will never be thanked enough for having found the words, which he named "the little voice", enabling us to hear again these injunctions. He reactivated these spiritual exercises so that we might once again "rise and walk", and advance in the process of our transformation. Someone arrives at Rutte with the aim of finding himself and lightening his load. He is presented with a whole gamut of exercises (drawing, aikido, dance, pottery, meditation) and applies himself assiduously to them. Then suddenly everything collapses and his ego rebels: "I told you so! This is no better than anyplace else! It's even worse!" He panics every time the door to mystery opens before him. If the therapist had simply kept to explanations, the ego comfortably lodged in its chair would have been better able to defend itself. But its barriers were evaded by the exercises, and the body perceived certain truths which are outside of the reach of the intellect. And in a very gentle way, at the heart of being, the "little voice" made itself heard: rise and walk, come and follow me.

It does not impose anything but the certainty that it brings new life is unlike any other. Durckheim and his colleagues awakened a new inner gaze. With a mixture of fear and wonder, people learn that their suffering are the manifestation of the mysterious process through which their being incarnates itself, that these sufferings have a meaning because their life has a meaning. These persons are reoriented and can begin to accept to make themselves co-operating witnesses to the Being which seeks to make itself flesh within them. The reactions of the intellect are quick, instantaneous. Those of the body take more time. The exercise inscribes itself in the body and goes on as long as necessary. There is often a delay: the intellect thinks it has understood and is impatient to find that the gestures of the body are still so awkward. But this very awkwardness is a mirror that the body turns on the intellect as long as necessary for the ego to convert itself. And as life cannot be fixed, we are never protected from falling into inertia!

Nothing which incarnates itself is ever definitively acquired. On the other hand, no downfall is ever definitively sealed. Even in the depths of despair and the feeling of meaninglessness, our body remains capable of repeating the simple and repetitive gestures which it has learned. The body and the exercise have their own logic and certainties. Durckheim loved to repeat: "It is in the moment when the exercise costs us the most and that we have the least desire to do it that it plays its greatest role and most merits its name as exercise." If it is truly practiced with the process of incarnation, not only will it lead us to the end of the night, but in our very night it will mysteriously accomplish its work. Many stages of our incarnation are related to germination ("If the seed does not fall in the earth and die, it cannot bear fruit...") which Hindu wisdom names "tamas." And in Latin, the word exercise evokes the fastidious training of athletes and soldiers. Certainly, our transformation into light has powerful moments which assist in regenerating energies: awakening, initial cleansing (or initiatory "baptism"), temptation, encounter with the Master, illumination...but it is not reduced to these striking moments. It only becomes fully itself in the duration of its long journey.

That is why the exercises are not a little clearing out process which we could do without, a concrete seduction to attract beginners. They must on the contrary accompany our transformation day by day, modifying us as often as necessary as they are both agents and verifiers of this transformation. In the Christian tradition, this work of transformation is called conversion. This is not a brief moment of lightning which disappears with the passage of time, a photo-souvenir in the back of a drawer. It can only be a never ending process, a costly purifier always to be taken up again. The conversion is "living" and upholds life only on condition of being practiced, exercised, "incarnated" every day. "Watch and pray": through these words, Jesus does not encourage us to go through some pious ideas or some nice feelings, but to change our life concretely.

INCARNATION AND THE DESCENT INTO HELL: TEMPTATION AND LETTING-GO

On these roads to Galilee, on this mountain of Transfiguration, on the road to Emmaus, Jesus "opened their heart to the meaning of Scripture and showed them that the Son of Man must suffer his passion..." and he made great effort to make them accept the unacceptable. It is only when all was consumed that they finally understood and entered the way in their turn. It is a great work to accept to open our eyes on that which tortures us: the instinct of preservation closes us up like an oyster. It is a great work then to unravel the torture which comes to us through external circumstances from those which engender our own terrors, both real and imaginary. It is a great work to finally accept this paradox: these sufferings guide us in spite of ourselves from our earliest childhood and yet we must accept the fact that we created them. How then do we untie these knots?

Taking up the Gospel and the other great Teachings, Durckheim helps us to find the meaning of this "passion". Everything occurs as though we had enveloped ourselves like mummies to protect ourselves against aggressions. And this more and more efficient protection ends by leading us to the edge of asphyxiation. We suffer perhaps from external aggressions, but they are disproportionate to the suffering which we inflict upon ourselves by desperately struggling in our mummification. We have often hardened and protected ourselves to push away aggressions which make us suffer, but it is also often to close our crooked fingers and our instincts of possession on a happiness which we do not want to let go of at any price. For a long time, these protections function well, more or less, even at the price of inconveniences, but the moment of explosion inevitably arrives. We feel this explosion in a confused way and we fear it as the catastrophe which will reduce to nothing that which we believe to be the work of our auto construction.

We feel ourselves besieged in our fortress and the stronger our temperament is strong the more our fortress is unassailable, and the more suffering accumulates: the explosion which breaks up a couple after twenty or thirty years of marriage, the stress which destroys an executive at the height of his responsibilities, the aged priest who sinks into alcoholism... That is when Jesus, all the great sages and Durckheim along with them, come to gently open the folded arms, the tight fists, the closed hearts by saying: no, this explosion will not be a catastrophe, far from it. A seed will rise, it is the growth of life. "But it is not at all what I was expecting!" Of course not! You were awaiting something closed in your defenses and you now descend into hell. But as long as you are alive, you are invited to resurrection. We can reveal the secret of reaching the depths of hell and returning to life: you only need to let go.

The phrase in the Our Father "do not lead us into temptation" could be translated as "Allow us to let go under temptation". When the initiatory exercises work properly, they make it possible for us to live a reduced model of this great temptation which is necessary to our incarnation. We relive one or the other of our crises by giving to the therapist the opportunity to say the word or accomplish the gesture which will open a first little breach for letting go. Often in the physical exercises, it is asked of us to "descend into our feet, our foundation," requests which most neophytes have trouble doing. It strikes them as a "gimmick" far from their problems. But it is on the contrary a wise teaching to begin to learn to let go on the corporal level through simple exercises. And it is these first efforts of letting go which will snowball and bring on the "debacle", the reduced model of the descent into hell, and at the very depths of this debacle, the liberating letting go. That is when the word temptation finds its greatest meaning.

It is comforting for believers to realize that this is a path which they share with Jesus. It is not surprising that those who approached Durckheim only out of intellectually curiosity were more or less disappointed. It is because they only saw him as other celebrities that he left merely a passing trace within them. They were not ready and their fortress was still impregnable. But for those who asked to be healed and who therefore include their bodies in the process, the doors of mystery open. The disciple must be ready for the Master to appear. And the disciple is ready when he or she begins to allow within him the mysterious alchemy of letting go. This is not a matter of one of those sessions of creativity as is often done nowadays and in which the participants have barely the time to experience certain new sensations. It is rather a matter of an engagement of one's whole being in a battle of life and death which the Zen tradition calls "passing through the wall." This is Jesus' demand to the rich man: "Leave all your possessions and follow me".

This is also the meaning of the Beatitudes: "Blessed are the poor, blessed are those who mourn." To enter into the Kingdom of God, the narrow door consists in crossing through the hell of poverty and the hell of tears: beyond this door we can begin to become somewhat transparent to the light of Being. We will have gone through the crucible as gold or silver which are purified.

INCARNATION IS A MYSTERY OF COMMUNION

Among the mirrors in which we can perceive a reflection of our image, there is of course the look of others. We have just stated to what extent, when this look is loving and creative, it is irreplaceable in awakening us to the world of Spirit and to the process of our incarnation. The encounter of others is one of the primordial dimensions which the body makes possible in our life. In a great number of cases, this encounter is lived in the mode of exchange: love and friendship, the relationship with the master or the therapist, etc. This exchange can also be involuntary. Sometimes a child teaches us through a naive reaction which is unimportant to him. The look which has revealed the depth of being to us is a look which we can hear, and it is on the level of the mystery of being that the relation is then established, if only for a few seconds. It is the light of our gaze which in turn nourishes the therapists and confirms them in their way. If the relation is capable of escaping the traps of transference, it truly becomes a companionship on the way.

The process of incarnation then is no longer a solitary and marginalizing journey because it occurs in the mystery of communion. At Rutte, this communion expresses itself among other things in the concern for maintaining the quality of the place, the objects, the gestures, the words, the silences...The respect for the presence of being is manifested: from the moment you enter, you perceive it, it surrounds you, it precedes the person who will greet you to assure you that she too is on the path of being and invites you to communion. This communion is the contrary of a seduction or a refuge! And of course, this communion is symbolized by the ritual of mediation in the zendo. The density of this silent communion is comparable to that of a monastery. Communion is not only the fruit of our physical and psychological needs, but comes from much farther, at the very horizons of the Spirit. Human relations are so fragile, so precious that we must receive them as a gift. To invoke pure coincidence would be thoughtless. For all those who have begun to advance on the path of being, communion appears as one of the most important revelations of the goal of their journey.

That is why the Christian tradition makes of communion the very definition of God: the mystery of the Trinity expresses this powerful image that God is love. We must remember that Jesus put at the center of his teaching the old biblical precept: "Love your neighbor as yourself." And that the Christian Churches have placed it at the center of their life through the rite of the sharing of the bread which they call "communion." In doing this, they say that they announce the death and resurrection of Christ until he returns: it is not so much a commemoration of a passed event as an expression of what occurs in the present in those who are on a journey toward being and who "accomplish in their bodies that which lacks in the passion of Christ" as saint Paul says. Communion is the feast of the incarnation. But the Christian Churches must remember that they do not have the monopoly over communion, no more than the one on the way to being or undergoing the process of incarnation. These are riches which they must share. For they also need to reach communion with all people to accomplish the mission which Jesus confides to them.

INCARNATION IS A GRACE AND OUR VOCATION IS TO RECEIVE IT

The incarnation of being within us is not conquered with clenched fists: we dispose ourselves to receive it each day and it is freely that it is given to us. An artist, at the height of his art after years of hard work, can be visited by grace on certain days. In his depths, he feels this event as a divine gift, a ray of being. For a moment, three graces are conjugated in him: the grace received at birth which make him choose his vocation, the grace elaborated by his persevering exercises and this fugitive grace, this lightning of harmony. It is an intense time which escapes analysis, and there are no words to describe it. A ray from beyond has pierced through his daily life. The artist who would refuse to recognize this third grace or to take it into account lacks a third dimension and this would be unfortunate for his art: by enclosing his creation only into the genius of his earthly person, he would become insane or sterile.

If we spectators are sensitive to this third grace, it is because we seek it when we come in contact with an "inspired author" or an "inspired interpreter". And the help of this inspiration comes to caress us in turn, pointing out the horizon of being for us once again. In conclusion, we find ourselves before an irresolvable paradox: the process of incarnation of our essential being requires time and a long, patient work and yet this essential being escapes the framework of time and space and gives itself to us only through grace. It does not obey our little existential self. All that participates in the mystery of life is made of polarities and it is from the tension between the poles that the energy is born. The two poles of the paradox do not cancel themselves, but make themselves mutually live. Our essential being is out of time, and that which demands to be incarnated, that which incarnates itself is already here, given from the beginning, born with us. "In the beginning was the Word" said saint John in the famous first words of his Gospel. "And not the image" add Jung and Durckheim.

The other traditions say: the Atman, the Spirit of Buddha, the Soul of the Universe, all these terms correspond to different cultures and mentalities but do not fully satisfy anyone since it is a mystery which they seek to evoke. Christians practice a ritual in which they impose their hands on the head of a brother or sister saying: "Receive the Holy Spirit". This means first of all that each generation recognizes itself as charged with transmitting the Holy Spirit to the following one through corporal gestures accompanied by a word, but that also means that the Holy Spirit is outside of time and accepts to come into the time of the one who opens himself in order to receive it. Perhaps it is enough in certain cases to let out the deep sighs of the miserable creature to receive it. But every human being is invited to rejoin the spirit: this depth of peace and of light which is overcome neither by age nor death, sin nor any other circumstance of our life, and which is the source of the light which seeks to radiate through our flesh.

The Zen Master insists that the meditator not leave this world during the time of meditation, and sometimes uses a stick to prevent it. He asks that the eyes not be closed, that he not sleep or dream, but rather cultivate a lucid and pacifying presence which holds the surrounding world at a proper distance. The meditator makes the effort to calm the whirlwind of thoughts and emotions which attack him day after day. At the moment when he despairs to achieve this, there suddenly appears the unexpected moment of grace, illumination, awakening. This moment can be ephemeral but it leaves a trace which will never be erased, and the meditator is incapable of analyzing how this sensation comes from beyond and at the same time from his own depths. This sensation is not the result of his reasoning nor reflections on holy Scriptures, even though this may have contributed to it.

This sensation is born from and in his waiting, a waiting very much alive since it requires a severe discipline of body and mind, but a waiting which explains nothing. Durckheim often reminded us of the definition of a circle: "The sky falls on the earth and if man can then die his death, all things can rediscover their original splendor." That which makes the circle a circle is the splendor of its central emptiness which is not a void. To meditate, we turn toward the emptiness which is not a void and which is our center and should not intimidate us. It disposes us to receive within us the eruption of grace, the moment when the Spirit comes to touch our sensitivity, making us feel that it incarnates itself within us and that our process of incarnation in well under way. Durckheim called these moments our "starry hours".

BECOMING REAL

THE NOTION OF ESSENTIAL BEING

by Pierre Erny

There is a central notion in the thought of Graf Durckheim: that of "essential being". It can be presented in six
propositions:

1. Our individuality as it is formed by hereditary transmission and influences from our environment, education
and history, does not explain the being whom we are. In
other words, we cannot be reduced to what we have become during the course of our life, to our existential self,
which our biography describes. This self certainly has its
own reality, but does not exhaust our reality. "Man goes
beyond man," said Pascal.

2. Beyond our biological and psychological make-up,
beyond our body and our soul, we carry within us the
possibility of tuning into a reality of an entirely different
order and to access a level of existence and of action
which infinitely transcends our ordinary experience.

3. This transcendent dimension which goes beyond our
biological--psychological--sociological self, is not merely added to our being like a free gift which is accidental
and supernatural. It is inherent, immanent, essential. We
are this dimension in the strongest sense of the term,
stronger even than when we say that we "are" our body

and our psyche. This dimension constitutes that which is most fundamental, most specific, most original, most permanent, most spontaneous, most free, most powerful within us. It acts within us as a principal of unity and co-hesion. It plunges us, as of now, into eternity and situates the changing being which we are in time and space, si-multaneously outside of time, space, and causality and their multiple conditionings and determinisms. It is this dimension which makes of us free persons, dressed in an absolute dignity, and not simple individuals; because of it, we can establish not only community, but communion.

4. This transcendent dimension of our being is not the product of a simple abstract metaphysical speculation. It can also become an object of experience which cannot be confused with any other, neither through its nature nor its intensity, nor through the feeling of fullness which ac-companies it, nor by its transforming effects. It can be prepared by a technique or an asceticism, or take place spontaneously, freely, sometimes brutally, offered then as the most precious of gifts.

5. This vital experience, through which can live and be deployed by that which lives in us, that which is most es-sential and most profound, is only rarely realized or felt by our consciousness. The transcendent dimension of our being which is its support represents a kind of paradise lost which we must find again. It appears to us as emi-nently fragile and is usually made esoteric, repressed, covered up, submerged, reduced to silence and to power-lessness by the products, agitations, and uprises of our mental life. As our inner cinema takes up all the room and makes too much noise, we are dissociated, cut off from our deepest and most transcendent roots. This ob-viously does not mean that on the ontological level, this dimension of our being is no longer present and active within us. But it is so in a purely underground manner,

without our conscious realization, and consequently without occupying its rightful place, without allowing it to re-establish balance and to introduce in our human experience enough to fertilize, vivify, illuminate from the interior, and transfigure it. It is always there, otherwise we would not be human, but hidden as though asleep. A part of us then disintegrates. We are beings who do not fully live, who limp along and cannot go very far, birds with only one wing turning in circles, ships which are not capable of deploying all their sails.

6. To call forth this transcendental experience, we must awaken or reawaken the dimension of our being, we might say the organ, which makes it possible. It must explode within us and break through the superficial crust of our conditioning. We can cultivate it, care for it, fortify it, not for itself because due to its transcendence we have no claim on it, but by getting rid of all that inhibits this eruption and manifestation. That which is an obstacle must "die" before being able to be reborn in a new form. In the hole we have just dug, this beyond within lives in our most intimate place and can now deploy itself and make us live on a level of which human beings generally know nothing.

Through these affirmations, which constitute the beginning point of the "initiatory therapy," Durckheim consciously rejoins the great spiritual traditions: --one way or the other, most of them are based on an anthropology according to which "man eats man". --they all admit the possibility of an experience which is of an entirely different order than ordinary physical or psyche experience. --the analysis of the obstacles to this experience prove that it is exceptional. --they all lead to the development of methods and the refinement of techniques whose aim is to facilitate them. In Durckheim's vocabulary, my essential self is that which I am in my depth, in my essence, that within which is linked to the Absolute and escapes all external influence, all contingency, all conditioning, the kernel of myself which roots me in Being and in the Divine. This notion can be understood in various ways according to the great historical traditions.

A HINDU READING

It is very easy to find this notion in the Vedanta. In its eyes, there is no other reality than Brahman, the divine All. To believe that we form a being in ourselves, with our own individuality, is to be lost in Maya, illusion. Individual being is only realized when we let the divine Self become transparent through us, if we erase ourselves in him. The Hindus call the immanent Brahman in human beings Atman (a word close to the German atmen, breathing). A very popular legend in India says that at the beginning human beings were gods. But they so abused their divine power that the supreme god decided to take it away from them and to hide it somewhere where they would not find it. He called together the other gods to ask their advice on where this hiding place might be.

Some said that it should be buried in the center of the earth, others suggested that it be thrown in the depths of the ocean. But knowing humanity, with its propensity and ability to search everywhere, they were not at all certain that one day it would be found. Before the perplexity of his advisers, Brahman said: "This is what we are going to do with the divinity of human beings: we will hide it in their depths, for that is the only place they will never think to look." Since then, humans travel, dig, plunge into the waters, search for something which is found in them... The spirituality of the Upanishads is based on this very strong statement: "You are That": in your depths you are god, and in developing this seed your whole being is called to become god.

A CHRISTIAN READING

Our own tradition cannot say that in the same terms, for it is based on the idea of creation ex nihilo which India does not ignore but which it has not valued in the same way. In our eyes, the creature is distinct from the Creator and has value in itself; it is not simple illusion. Nevertheless, there is a sentence in the Gospel which states: "The Kingdom of Heaven is within you." This can mean: "among you" but also: "at the center or in the depths of your being." There is also a sentence which is found throughout the patristic tradition: with different nuances, it is found in the writings of Ireaneus of Lyon, Athanasius of Alexandria, Augustine of Hippo, suggesting that the early Christians must have intensely meditated upon it: "God became man so that man might become god."

In the end, this is also what the Christian tradition proposes: deification, theomorphosis, transformation, transmutation in God. One might say quite appropriately that Hindu mysticism is a mysticism of unity, the recognition of our fundamental unity with the Divine, merely veiled and obscured by the fact that we prefer the illusion of the present world, while Christian mysticism is a mysticism of union, in the matrimonial meaning of the word, a union which retains a distinction, where each remains what he is, which does not lead to identification but to a fusion without confusion. The biblical theme of wedding refers to God and Israel, to Christ and the Church, and to humans and their Creator. The biblical and Judeo-Christian sensitivity is not that of the Vedanta. Two observations must be made concerning this fact. First, what can be said in this area can only be inadequate and a miserable approximation.

How could we believe that a formula, because it satisfies the games of the intellect, is finally closer to a reality which in any case is inexpressible and cannot be put into formulaes? That which touches the depths of things can

be approached only through myths with multiple interpretations or through koans whose paradoxical meanings
require one to go beyond purely intellectual categories.
The ex nihilo creation is a mystery which transcends our
understanding and if we seek to rise to a state of contemplation from a purely conceptual and verbal solution we
will discover how much the pantheist or emanational traditions have to offer. Secondly, can we conceive of a
union if between the two terms there is not already a certain natural unity beyond the distinctions which is more
fundamental than the differences? For a rather trivial
comparison, can we conceive of a union between a may-
bug and a dragonfly or between an elephant and a croco-
dile? Obviously not because these are different species
which have nothing in common.

However, there is a possible union between man and
woman because it is based on a common humanity. How
can we conceive of a union between that which is human
and that which is divine if in humanity the divine is not
already present in one way or another, and moreover if in
the divine humanity is not already present in one way or
another, if between the two there is not already a connaturality, a secret union? In every being there is a triple
aspect: --first, the reference to a source, an origin, a be-
getting; --next, that which is its nature, its essence, and
gives it shape and meaning, the law which structures and
orders it from within; --finally, that which gives it its life,
its soul, its breath, its ability to act and to transform itself, that which integrates it in a unity and harmony
which transcends it. In this triple aspect, every being is a
reflection of the Trinitarian God.

In Christian language: --the Father is the Source, the
original Fullness; --the Son is the Logos, the Word, the
Idea according to which creation is realized, its internal
Law, that which gives it form; --and the Spirit is the

Pneuma, Life, that which animates, uplifts, vivifies, and provides the impulse for the forces of union and love in all things. In primitive Christian theology, with Ireaneus of Lyon especially, there is reference to the two hands of God, the Son- Word-Logos and the Spirit-Breath-Pneuma. And it is always in conjunction with these two hands that God acts. To understand the reality of "essential being", we can refer successively to these two aspects.

THE MAN-WORD

In an anthropomorphic language we can say that God creates in relation to an idea, a thought, a drawing, a project, therefore of an inner word, a logos. Thomas Aquinas defined the idea as the form or the model which the artist contemplates in order to produce the exterior work which he has in mind. The builder, for example, conceives in his spirit the form of the house to be built. In Christian philosophy it is classic to represent to one-self the platonic ideas, the immutable and eternal models, the "Urbilder" of things here below, as divine thoughts forming in a way the architectural plan of the universe. In the hierarchy of creatures, human beings have an eminent place aside, due to our free will, the reflection of the divine freedom, which on one hand approaches ontologically to God, but on the other allows us to turn away and to refuse the destiny which is assigned to us.

Our essential being is first of all that which God wanted us to be, the idea which He had of us from all eternity. Every type of being, but also every creature considered in its singularity, is related to an idea and to a divine project: --their nature and essence correspond to the idea --their destiny, mission, that which they are called to, their vocation corresponds to the project. Each being is therefore a logos, a word made flesh in a precise time and place, a manifestation of the eternal and divine logos. Mutatis mutandis must be said of every being, and emi-nently of human beings, and which is said of Christ. He is mysteriously present in every creature, right into his ultimate mystery of death and resurrection. To be convinced of this, we only need to look at nature, the living beings and their growth and development, humanity in its psychic and spiritual life: everything is dominated by the law of "stirb und werde", "die and become", as Goethe described it.

All the ancient mysteries, all the traditional ritual initiations, were scenes of the passage from death to new life. For if the Word is in the person of Christ a historical being, it is also a cosmic reality which is at work in all things from the beginning to the end of the world. He has always taught persons , worked their consciences and raised up the great spiritual traditions which ultimately rejoin each other despite their obscurities, their deviations and their unconsciousness. The first Christians spoke of the logos spermatikos, the word in the state of germination or seed.

MAN-SPIRIT

Let us consider now the aspect of pneuma. The idea of spirit has become one of the most confused ideas in philosophy. The manuals and dictionaries of Western theology speak abundantly of the soul and of the Holy Spirit, but very rarely of the spirit of human beings. Yet saint Paul often spoke of the "nous" or the "pneuma" and attributed them to humanity. What Graf Durckheim called "essential being" joins that which the biblical tradition called the spiritual, "pneumatic" dimension of human beings. In the Hebraic Bible, "ruah" (translated by "pneuma", then "spiritus"), is the wind, the breath, the vital dynamism of the person, the animating and vivifying principle, the divine breath which man received according to Genesis: "the Lord made man with the dust of the earth, then breathed into his nostrils the breath of life." Even if certain texts allow some doubt, Paul clearly distinguishes human pneuma and divine pneuma, our spirit and the Spirit of God.

The former points to the latter which inhabits the believer, guides him, takes hold of him as of old it took hold of the prophets, makes of him an adoptive son, allows him to call God Abba, "Father", manifests itself in mysterious phenomena, outside of human possibilities (pneumatika, charismata). Understood in this way, the spirit is always ek tou theou, "issued from God". It belongs to the divine sphere; in the human being, it is of the order of a reality received from above; it comes from God and returns to God; it puts in relief the relationship between human beings and God; an eschatological gift, it attests to humanity that it is destined for the resurrection; a transcendent element, it is for humans and in humans the manifestation of the Divine; it roots us in Being, Life, the Absolute; it is a seed within us, a divine spark.

APPROACHES AND STAMMERING

When we admit, with the neo-Platonists, that the world is issued from God through successive emanations until it reaches its ultimate limit which is matter, we have no trouble in admitting that we are made of the divine essence, though certainly degraded, and that we can climb the cascade up to the source in its unity. When, on the other hand, we admit with biblical thought, that the universe is created ex nihilo, it remains necessarily distinct from God, and no creature can be divine. The relationship is then more subtle and infinitely more mysterious. We can nevertheless suggest certain approximations. God can only act in relation to what He is. *Agere sequitur esse,* said the scholastics, "we act in relation to what we are". It is inevitable that we find ourselves intimately in our behavior and actions. The painting is distinct from the painter, and yet it reveals something of the artist.

The universe created by God cannot not be in his image. As God infinitely transcends his creature, something of this transcendence must necessarily be found within it. We could also say that the world is like a mirror in which is reflected the divine splendor, like a planet lit by the light of the sun which would be lost in infinity and darkness without it. There is a connaturality between emitted light and reflected light. The problem is that there are images which do not resemble each other much and that there are bad mirrors. The work of humanity, that which is proper to us as bearers of freedom, is to make the image resemble its source more and more and to polish the mirror to allow it to reflect the light with always more efficiency and fidelity, all the while being conscious that a reflection will never be equal to reality. This is the fundamental theme of the theology of deification: that which is an image must tend toward an always more perfect resemblance. We could also say that our spirit is divine in depth, negatively, that it is like the left-over impact, the imprint from the divine breath. It is within us as the "organ" of the divine.

Certainly, the eye is not light, and the ear is not sound; but they could never be organs of light and sound if they did not have a certain affinity and connaturality with it. Here we could say some very interesting things about the symbolism of numbers, as does for example Jewish mysticism concerning the story of Creation. When we pass from the one to the two, then to the three, we completely change the register. The two is not the one, and yet in the two the one is mysteriously, truly present as the seed in the egg. We could also say that a point, a line, a surface, a volume are not the same thing. And yet, in all of them, the point is mysteriously present. God and His creatures belong to completely different orders, and yet in the creature, God is mysteriously present. He is present in every creature, but especially in human beings who are the recapitulation of creation.

The spirit, in the biblical sense, is not a thing nor a being. It is this mysterious divine presence within us which makes us human and at the same time more than human. It is through the spirit, our spirit, that we have a certain acquaintance, a certain contact, a certain connaturality, a certain affinity, a certain resemblance, a certain familiarity, a certain intimacy, a certain participation with God Himself. Since God is outside of time, space and all external influence, and is supreme energy, total freedom, eternal youth, perfect joy, unshakeable firmness, infinite tenderness, it is through the spirit which is within us that we can also experience what is freedom, joy, strength, love, youth which never vanishes, energy which nothing can overcome. The spirit presented in this way is of a completely different order than the soul. The spiritual dimension of persons is articulated in his psychic and physical dimension but must be clearer distinguished from it. This distinction can go as far as antithesis. Indeed, when the soul is vacated by the spirit to the extent that it is no longer turned to God, it nourishes itself of the body and materializes itself.

On the other hand, if the spirit plunges into God, it carries the soul with it which, in turn, carries the body along, and the two become spiritualized completely. In saying that the spirit thus conceived is inherent in the very nature of humanity, we make the notions of supernatural useless and obstructive. Our true nature is that of the original Adam, dressed in the only light and living in total familiarity with God; it is that of the "second" Adam, the Christ, when on Mount Tabor or on Easter morning he appeared as he is, without veils, in his divine-humanity, completely transfigured by the Spirit, completely penetrated and illuminated by it, tangibly spiritualized and deified, body and soul. It is to this that we are destined by our nature.

BECOMING REAL

While we await this, we struggle in states beneath our nature. But we already carry within our "body of glory", we
need only let it break through, let it explode the walls
which holds it in, and the history of the saints shows us
that some persons have achieved this while still alive.
We witness here the different viewpoint from that of the
position of current theology. The Christ does not come to
take us in a natural state to raise us to a supernatural
state. He comes to join us in our "hell," in our misery as
half-persons, of stunted, extinguished beings, there precisely where we are the weakest, the most threatened,
there where it hurts most, to restore us to our original nature, but this time freely taken up. Finally, the notion of
the "heart" is important for the Bible and the Tradition,
depicting the place where essential being links up with
the existential self, where the transcendent dimension of
the person erupts from within, pierces through us, and
around which it is possible to progressively unify ourselves.

CONCLUSION

The insights which Graf Durckheim offers concerning
"essential being" are surprisingly similar to those which
Nicolas Berdiaev says of the spirit. Here are some excerpts from "Spirit and Reality", published by Berdiaev
in 1943: "The spirit is not a different reality from the
body and the soul; it does not proceed from an object, but
from God, who is subject. It is like the breath of God
which penetrates us and confers on us his supreme dignity, the supreme quality of his existence, freedom and
inner unity." "The spirit is not being, but the meaning of
being, the truth of being. It is the divine element in human beings. It is the spirit which makes us in the image
of God. It is thanks to the spirit that we can rise to the
highest divine spheres." "The spirit is not created by God

the way nature is, but rather emanates from God. It is poured out, breathed into us by God."

"The spirit is both transcendent and immanent. In it the transcendent becomes immanent and the immanent transcendent." "That which characterizes the spirit is total independence in relation to natural and social determinisms. It is the inner as opposed to the external." "It is in our spirit that the Holy Spirit acts. The spiritual life is a communion with the divine life. In our greatest depths, it is revealed that that which occurs within us occurs in the very depths of the divine life." "All charismatas, all gifts come from the spirit, not only the gifts of the prophets and of the apostles and the saints, but also those of the poets, the philosophers, the inventors, and the reformers." "We do not have an objective spiritual nature over and above our corporal and psychic nature.

But our soul and our body can have access to another level, a higher level, that of spiritual existence, that of freedom, opening onto the kingdom of meaning." "Our body can therefore participate with the spirit, be spiritualized and conquered for our liberty. It is with our body that we can reach theosis, the entrance into the divine life." "The spirit is not a different reality, but gives meaning to reality." "Through the spirit, God is rooted in human beings and we are rooted in God." "It is through the spirit that we receive everything from God and give everything to God." We know that in his writings, Durckheim has not always gone to the end of his positions. It seems to me that in these few sentences, Berdiaev joins the deep thought of the sage of the Black Forest.

BECOMING REAL

THE TRINITARIAN VISION OF REALITY

by Willi Massa

The question which ultimately preoccupies Durckheim is the following: how can the experience of supernatural Being transform man in such a way that his terrestrial form can manifest the radiance of divine Being? This question makes of him a prophet of a spirituality of the inner way, based on experience of Being. It leads to the transformation of man and reaches its culminating point in the liberating awakening of Being. The departure point of this question, the genesis of his thought, is always the great experience which, in human existence, manifests the quality of Being beyond space and time. Is this a dimension which is that of the great Life or only of its purely individual reflection? This is determined by the "evidence of the "taste", by the "quality of radiance" and by its "power of transformation".

There is an unquestionable "taste" of the numinous which attests to the presence of another reality in human consciousness. No word can describe it, no category can imprison it. A particular radiance is perceived. Finally, the proof of the validity of the experience of Being is the degree of transformation which it produces. It brings the power to support existence and makes possible a certain way of acting in the world. In Christian language, we would say that this growth in man incarnates itself, and is a process of manifestation of the divine image in human consciousness which is also visible in our behavior.

THE EXPERIENCE OF THE TRINITARIAN UNITY OF LIFE

In the starry hours of life, in the most serious trials as in the happiest moments, we encounter the experience of the Great Life. "These are moments when we are touched by something deeper which suddenly introduces us into another reality. It can touch us in the darkness of despair like a light which transforms everything around us. It can come to us at the summit of happiness and give everything a supernatural brilliance. Each time we come upon our point of rupture and reach the limits of our strength, of our reason or of our psychic endurance, if we accept this annihilation and receive it as the most fundamental thing in us, something new will be born."

In this experience, invisible Being appears to our consciousness as an invincible power, primordial meaning and unconditional love in which everything is contained. Power, meaning, love: these are the three qualities of Life in its unity. A third experience allows us to speak of a Life present beyond time and space. "A person can suddenly feel himself surrounded, carried in invisible arms, secretly protected, not knowing who loves him or whom he loves. He now feels sheltered by a supernatural love." In moments of great joy, the doors of immanent consciousness can open and reveal this Being with its inexhaustible plenitude, its light and universal law which gives form and meaning to all things. We also feel its unity which places everything in the harmony of a universal love.

THE KEY TO THE TRINITARIAN EXPERIENCE OF ONENESS

"The voice of divine Being always resonates within us. We must learn how to tune ourselves to it, like instruments, in order to respond to it." Tuning the instrument means: Trust life, renounce security, listen to the voice of depth in your essential Being. Then the existential self is vanquished in its narrowness and fear. A door opens and invites us to go out into the vastness of indestructible Life. Human maturity takes root in this trust. We have reached maturity when we renounce the will of the existential self and align our will with the requirements of essential Being. In this essential Being is found the secret of Life which creates, orders, and liberates.

1) "The reflection of Being in life always expresses Life as undivided fullness which maintains and regenerates everything." This fullness is perceived as the ground which supports us, as the source from which everything arises, as the power where our trust and strength take root and which nothing can destroy.

2) The reflection of Being always indicates the essential meaning which transcends all reason. The living, unfathomable order, which is beyond the meaning and meaninglessness of the world, penetrates our intimate consciousness. "When the feeling of depth opens within us, we are suddenly filled with the mystery of a fullness whose wealth is infinite. Above all, we feel it as the individuality of our own core. We feel it as the duty of entering upon the path, undetermined by the world. The meaning and goal of the way, whatever its direction in the world, is always the manifestation of Being in life." The reflection of Being brings to our consciousness the One which contains all things and manifests itself as love. Therefore the level of evolution of the human being is seen in the power of his love.

BECOMING REAL

THE MANIFESTATION OF THE TRINITARIAN REALITY REFLECTED IN THE CORPORAL FORM

The trinity of Life appears in the trinity of posture, tension and breathing. We always incarnate a certain attitude. We are either rooted or outside of our center of gravity. We also express a certain tension between form and dissolution. A balanced relationship creates a rhythm with breathing: we give and we receive. There is creation of form and surrender to the depths of the One. Essential Being, which is participation with divine Being, expresses itself through the whole of life and therefore on the corporal level. When we live in contradiction with the yearning of our essential Being, with our inner requirement of form and promise of unity, we live against ourselves, against our order and our health. "The center of blockage which affects the whole person is found in the self which opposes the movement of transformation toward which essential Being tends."

To work to liberate these physical blockages is to develop the capacity for transparence. "We must acquire through this work a fundamental attitude of body and spirit through which perturbations -- which no one is spared from -- do not block the action of the Spirit but call upon its unifying, regenerating force." To the extent that attitude, tension and breathing are done consciously and responsibly, they become the beginning point and the place of a manifestation of Being where we find our true selves. When our tension is placed in our center, it maintains a deep elasticity which keeps us from all blockage." The assurance of our attitude expresses a true confidence. Holding oneself straight, which is both a sign of dignity and modesty, and a free breathing, allowing us to receive and to give are the manifestation of Life, the ground which supports us, the formative power and movement which unites us.

The biblical expression "Glorify God with your body" finds its meaning here. "The characteristic of a right attitude is to make us constantly able to go out into the world without tension and to receive it as it is because we are transparent to essential Being, capable of bearing witness to it in all circumstances with suppleness, serenity and goodness." Right attitude, which is the proper way of being present in the world, is therefore found in the triad of posture, breathing and tension. All three should be transparent to the divine Being present in the essential Being of man. "If he is 'vertical' in the right way, this posture links through its attitude heaven and earth. His link with the lower does not endanger his verticality and the latter does not represent a rejection of his attachment to the earth. The "lower" with which he is in contact is like the roots of a tree which are not opposed to the ascending growth but rather assure it.

This aspiration toward the higher is not a tearing away from the earth for it is at the same time the power of rooting which generates the ascending movement. The right way of manifesting the relation of the high with the low expresses the fact that man is both linked to the earth and attracted to the sky, nourished and carried by the earth and at the same time reaching for the sky." When our way of being corresponds to the relationship with the world of humanity, nature and things which is our destiny, it means that "we are both closed and open, in a transparent contact, separated and at the same time linked to the world, reserved and open toward it." In right relation with ourselves, we are in an attitude which is both relaxed and withheld.

THE TRINITARIAN ASPECTS OF THE EXERCISE ON THE WAY

The Trinitarian structure corresponds to a triple realization on the way of transparence. The triple quality of Life, which seeks to penetrate human consciousness, to

97

manifest itself in it so that it may lead us to our fulfillment and our capacity to love, corresponds to the three
fundamental aspects of spiritual exercise:

1) to perceive Being (become conscious of it);

2) to remain within it (let it take its place);

3) to melt into Being (become one with it). a) The perception of Being breaks down the wall of the
consciousness focused on the object and allows us to be
touched by the inexpressible. The contact requires that
we completely accept it because it cannot be grasped by
rational consciousness. The call of Being imperatively
demands listening and obedience. b) Remaining in Being
allows transcendence to increase in our consciousness. It
gains force which creates form, light and order. c) Then
comes the invitation which is a promise of receptivity into the unity of Life. A new person is born. He no longer
thinks of living through himself but only through the
"beyond."

THE TRINITY OF BEING AND THE CHRISTIAN TRINITY

"The Trinity is not a privilege of Christianity. There is no
religion without the Trinity. The Christian Trinity is a
Christian way of picturing the Trinity of Being: Fullness,
Law and Unity, that is, the Father, Son, and Holy Spirit.
In Buddhism, we speak of Buddha, Dharma, Samgha. In
Hinduism, you have Brahma, Vishnu, Shiva. In Shin-
toism, you have the saber to express power, the mirror to
express the law and that famous chain, that jewel which,
with its suppleness, represents the gentleness of love." In
the great Life there is no immobility. "Movement always
leads from the Father to the Son and from the Son
through the Holy Spirit it returns back to the Father.

The Trinity is a movement, the eternal movement, the mysterious movement in which we all participate as living beings. Nothing exists outside of the Holy Trinity and each living being is an image of it. Life becomes Form, and the dynamic Unity which is at the basis of everything that is living links all things; nothing exists outside of the Holy Trinity because everything is within in. When this Life leaves, things decompose, and a human body turns to dust when it is no longer inhabited by the Life." Here the Christian faith in the Trinity becomes the deepest revelation of our Being and the vision of our future form. It finds its summit in its transparence to the Trinitarian Life secretly present within it.

Durckheim found this idea realized in Jesus. "It is not Buddha who is the center of my life but the Christ, the one who calls from the depths of our being, the one who is in us like an immanent transcendence, the living Christ. With the one whom the Orient calls Buddha, he is supernatural, universal Being within us. The difference is that, not only must we annihilate the self to remain in the Buddha, but in Christ we become a new person, witness to the immanent transparence present in our core. We become a son in the way that it is meant in the Gospel of Thomas: "You must find me in you, then you will become conscious that you are sons of God."

In Jesus, the Great Life opens the eyes of humanity for the first time, not only through our inner consciousness of God but through the duty of becoming a witness, that is, to fulfill in our human form the divine spark within us. That is why Jesus calls himself the new Adam. In Jesus, the Christ has taken on a human form. The Christ who says of himself: "Before Abraham was, I am." Thus begins a new age in the history of humanity."

BECOMING REAL

ACCEPTING THE UNACCEPTABLE

by Arnaud Desjardins

One of the major themes in the teaching and writings of Karlfried Graf Durckheim is that of "the acceptance of the unacceptable". In Meditating -- Why and How we read: "The more a person finds himself in a situation or an agony which seems unacceptable, the closer he is to the possibility of an initiatory experience, if he admits to the fundamental rule which is required in these cases: the acceptance of the unacceptable. Then the opportunity is offered to take a step forward, to rise one step higher or even to break through a wall. The more the impasse is narrow and a dead end, the more the leap becomes indispensable. We are dealing with a dead end. Should we accept that which is a dead end? Not only must we accept it, but we must enter into the uttermost part of the dead end. This is a paradoxical requirement! But in it is found transcendental truth."

In "The Breakthrough of Being", Graf Durckheim writes: "The transcendent embraces us when we finally have the courage not to retreat before great suffering, but on the contrary that we accept to let ourselves be consumed by it, filled with faith in that which awaits us beyond the void that frightens us in the moment...In the same way, the one who is broken, destroyed by an absurd event will know the reality of Being, thanks to the "experience", and will be able in an instant full of grace, to accept it. Through it he will feel, in a sudden manner, a deep meaning coming from another dimension. Finally, the knowledge of Being is given to those who have lost everything and, finding themselves in the most complete solitude, are capable of accepting it. It is at that very moment that, in unexpected fashion, from the depths of their complete destitution that there comes the unsuspected grace which makes them feel surrounded, protected and vivified with a love that is not of this world."

THY WILL BE DONE

Even though in his writings Durckheim does not refer explicitly either to the God of Abraham or of Moses nor to the Jesus of the Gospels, this acceptance--this yes without restriction to personal drama and tragedies--is no different from what the Christians have understood as submission to the will of God or surrender to the Providence of God. It joins the fundamental theme to "do the will of God". The Christ said: "I have not come into the world to do my will but to do the will of the One who sent me" and again: "Thy will be done".

Every Christian knows that here resides the very essence of Christianity. Yet, when he think of this attitude "to have no other will than the will of God" as witnessed to by all the mystics, the Christian most often has the impression that "to do the will of God" only means to act according to the will of God. This approach therefore concerns action. Unfortunately, people who claim the will of God, whether at the heart of Christianity or of Islam, have been capable in the name of this so-called divine will of making other persons suffer in a thousand different ways and especially, in the name of this will, to openly violate other commandments formulated in the Holy Books.

From one point of view, the history of Christianity and of Islam is a long series of crises, tortures, injustices, exploitation and oppression, untiringly bought back by the splendor of the saints and the faith of the anonymous faithful. On the other hand, there has always existed in Christianity another understanding of this submission to the will of God which does not concern our actions but consists in seeing the will of God toward us in all the events of our existence. That is where is found the vital idea without which ordinary understanding of wanting to do the will of God loses its meaning. This conviction that everything which happens to us is wanted by God is confirmed and enlightened by an entirely different way of expressing oneself, which is non-dualistic, demands the recognition of that which is and not the superimposing of that which ought to be.

There has certainly been among believers clear difficulties revealed by the questions which have been asked to Christian spiritual masters for two thousand years. How can God, who is justice and goodness, want the acts which seem to us criminal and contrary to what we consider to be His own commandments expressed through the prophets or through Christ? The Christian tradition has always answered: "it is not the will of God that he who is in error remain in error; it is not the will of God that he who makes his neighbor suffer remain on this level of egoism, cynicism and cruelty but, for you who feel yourselves victim of an injustice, that is God's will for you. Can we still accept today this way of expressing ourselves? I don't know. But if we open ourselves to this understanding which is perfectly in accord with the other spiritual or esoteric teachings, then Christianity becomes truly liberating.

Accepting the unacceptable is a very good formula. If we accept that which, in the end, seems acceptable although unfortunate or bothersome, that is not what will allow us a true rupture on the inner level, or the passage to a whole other level of feeling and understanding. If we accept that which seems to us unacceptable, not as a defeat but as an active attitude which is victorious over our habitual ways of reacting, then a very great realization can open before us. To accept the unacceptable and to accept the incomprehensible--which is perhaps even more difficult--that before which reason rebels: "That is not possible!" These are times when we cannot understand how certain persons, either individually or collectively, have been able to behave in such a way, especially when this behavior affects us directly. We must not try to understand at first, but only later.

First we must accept, understanding will come later. Through this acceptance, we move beyond the mental, beyond even ordinary intelligence. And we know that the Greek word "metanoia"--which we normally translate as repentance--means "to go beyond the usual intellect". It is a revolutionary way to see, to think, to understand and to judge--and especially not to judge. It is this submission to the divine will which has created Christian mysticism. We could compose an anthology of witness from the saints in this regard. They have all followed the example of the submission of the Virgin Mary. To the Angel who announces to her this incredible news that she will be pregnant by the Holy Spirit, she answers with a wondrous simplicity: "I am the handmaid of the Lord, let it be done according to Your word".

We can feel, that even if the Angel had told her: "You see, Mary, this little bump on your breast is cancer and in one year you will be dead"--in the same way she would have answered: "I am the handmaid of the Lord, let it be according to Your Word." Therefore, from the origin of Christianity, that is, since the beginning of the Gospel which is Mary's yes to Christ's ultimate acceptance "that this cup be taken from me, but let it be done according to your will", all the greatest Christians have lived this fusion of their will with the divine will, understood as an adherence to circumstances, to the most concrete events, from moment to moment, including all that seems diabolical or satanic. We must insist on this final point: if we begin to decide that such or such a behavior has nothing to do with the will of God but that it is only a matter of the will of Satan, of the Sly One, we will never get out of the world of conflict. In everything that would happen to us and not correspond to our own vision of good and to our ideologies, we would feel justified in refusing it, in becoming indignant, in rebelling by considering it not to be the will of God but only that of the demon.

The testimonies of the mystics, from the celebrated works to the least known works, confirm this confidence: to see not the will of the "Prince of this World", but that of God in the most unjust acts which may have victimized us. But that is also what has nourished the faith and inner freedom, the serenity and joy of thousands and probably millions of anonymous Christians who have lived their existence in this light.

CONFIDENCE IN DIVINE PROVIDENCE

Other than the famous texts of Meister Eckhart and the Fathers of the ancient Church, Gregory of Nyssa, Clement of Alexandria, and outside of catholic mystical writings, I have had two little pamphlets by my bedside. One is entitled "Confidence in the Divine Providence". It is written by a little known author, Jean-Baptiste Saint-Jure, of the Company of Jesus, and it is said that it was the favorite reading of the priest of Ars. The certainty which inspires this little book is extremely simple: if you see in everything that happens to you the will of God and if you wish for all that happens to you because you cannot have any other will than the will of God, you will reach happiness here below. This is obvious. As happiness is the correspondence between that which I want and that which occurs, if instead of requiring that the world correspond to my expectations, I put myself in harmony with the world, the result is exactly the same; there is a correspondence and no longer conflict or frustration.

I share with you several excerpts: "There is the secret of happiness on earth: to correspond to the will of God." "To see God in all things; in all things, to submit to the will of God." A little further, a citation from the Old Testament justifies this attitude. God says to Moses: "It is I who makes die and I who make live, I bless and I heal." And further, we read: "We must, on his word, believe that in all the different kinds of events nothing happens except by his order or his permission." These sentences all go in the same direction: to affirm that it is always the will of God which is at work and not sometimes His will and sometimes the will of Satan. This way of seeing the will of God even in the actions said to be perverse of those who seek to do us evil is obviously linked to the act of forgiving and loving one's enemies. This relationship is clear: "We must not stop at the passions of those to whom God has given power over us to make us suffer, nor worry about their malicious intentions toward us and keep ourselves from all aversion against them." Or again: "Our interest should lead us to greet rather than push away their attempts since they are actually the attempts of God Himself."

This doctrine has always been familiar to souls truly illuminated by God as is seen in the famous example of the saintly Job. He lost his children and his possessions, fell from wealth into misery and said: "The Lord gave me everything, the Lord took it all away; as it pleased the Lord, so it happened, blessed be the name of the Lord." Saint Augustine observed: "See how Job does not say -- "The Lord gave it to me and the demon took it away," but rather: It is the Lord who gave me my children and my possessions and it is He who took them away."

This Christian approach is based on the conviction that for each of us God acts as a father who is only motivated by his love for his children, and who only wishes to teach them in order to little by little make them his equals. It is written in the Gospel "be perfect as your Father in heaven is perfect." Many simple examples are given concerning this. They are found in every religion. The little child who is wounded does not understand why his mother places iodine on his cut because it burns, but it is with love that his mother imposes upon him this temporary suffering. In the old days, medication was not made of easy to swallow capsules, but bitter poisons and the child who had to take them could not understand how his mother could be so cruel while she is acting only for his own good.

We read in Saint Augustine: "Let us never attribute either to demons or to men but to God the true source of our losses, our displeasures, our afflictions, our humiliations. To act otherwise, observed Saint Dorothy, would be to imitate the dog who discharges his anger on the rock instead of turning it on the hand that threw it. Therefore, keep yourself from saying: this person is the cause of the trouble which I am experiencing, he is the author of my ruin. Your ills are not the work of this man but of God. Be assured that God does everything with the deepest wisdom and for holy and sublime ends." Even if the vocabulary is out of fashion today, these simple truths -- some would say simplistic-- have animated and transfigured millions of Christians, Sufis, and Hindus on a devotional path considered "dualist".

BECOMING REAL

An idea which often recurs in this approach is that God makes us suffer while considering us -- that is the expression that I have often found in this kind of text -- as noble creatures. Noble creatures are creatures with a certain courage. God honors us by not considering us only as weak, infantile, whining creatures only capable of complaining, but as beings of courage and dignity, capable of facing trials in order to grow and to progress. "The Lord chastises those He loves and flagellates those whom He admits among His children." This clinging to the will of God is expressed by the word "submission." And when we say "submission to the will of God," we must understand another expression which is less well known: the identification of our will and the will of God.

The word "submission" can resonate wrongly within us and give us the impression of a failure or defeat. But if we wish to admit that God is at work everywhere and decide that we wish what God wants, we are not capitulating before God but make ourselves equal with Him by rising to his level. It would be even more correct to call it the "non-distinction of our will and of the will of God" or the "fusion of our will with the will of God, even in the unacceptable, even in the incomprehensible." This reminds me of the words of a Hindu sage in the nineteenth century who affirmed: "May Your will be done does not yet express an ultimate truth. The ultimate truth is always my will is done because my will has become that of God and is completely intermingled with it." Here intervenes the fundamental theme of yes and no. Master Eckhart has said: ""It is the no which burns in hell."

The consciousness of separation, the fundamental error, begins with the no. But of these "no's" the first is probably the refusal of the baby, especially if his birth was in the least traumatic. It is the no which created the ego, it is the no which has created the mental. Only the yes can

108

dissolve the ego. You know the famous word of Saint Paul: "Christ was not yes or no. He was only YES."

FROM DISOBEDIENCE TO SUBMISSION

We can see how a few simple truths can be transformative and liberating. This "yes" which is linked to an idea which impregnated all Christianity but has often been misunderstood and which is considerably rejected today and is the one of obedience and disobedience. At the beginning, disobedience, in the Christian meaning of the word, means to disobey God and, consequently, to distance ourselves more and more from peace, sinking always deeper into error. But to disobey God does not only imply the transgression of a commandment either of the Old Testament or of Christ, but is first of all to refuse that which is. In order to move from a moral level to a more interior, esoteric level, let us remember this vital point. The first disobedience, or the fundamental sin, is to refuse relative reality, to no longer agree with God who is responsible for all that occurs to me, including that which does not correspond with my egocentric and subjective perspective. And obedience begins with saying yes to that which is. Then obedience to such and such a commandment can find its place.

But it only appears as a consequence of that first obedience. To refuse all day long that "what is, be" and to refuse that the unacceptable or the incomprehensible be, is disobedience. To permit this disobedience, arguing over reality or rejecting it as the will of Satan, and later imagining that we are going to do the will of God because we are going to try to apply certain commandments, cannot constitute an evolving and liberating Christianity. This attitude can only lead to all the impasses abundantly described by those who have formulated often justified critiques of a Christianity not as Christ proposed to us but as it has been lived. Obedience helps to fuse our individual will with the divine will.

How could a musician be at ease and happy if, in a great orchestra, he refused to play the part directed by the conductor and interpreted by his colleagues? He could only struggle in his discomfort.

In the little book by Saint Alphonse, The Will of God, written around 1775, the same ideas are taken up with the same conviction: "We must unite our will with all that God does. When we wish for nothing except that which God wants, then the divine wish becomes our wish. The difficulty is to receive the will of God in all events gracefully, whether or not it satisfies our instinctive desires. God does not want the sin of the one who offends us, but God nevertheless wishes our humiliation, our poverty, our mortification." And he states: "Of all that happens to him, nothing is cause for sadness," a verse taken from the book of Proverbs, a little seed which could just as well be Buddhist as Christian. Saint Alphonse also quotes from Ecclesiastes: "The senseless, says the Holy Spirit, is changing like the moon while the righteous man, in his wisdom, remains equal to himself like the sun." The text further adds: "The senseless,that is the sinner, changes like the moon which grows today and decreases tomorrow.

Today, you see this person laugh, tomorrow he will cry; today, he is meek and mild and tomorrow he will be a raging tiger. Why is this? Because his tranquility depends on changing events, sometimes pleasant, sometimes unpleasant. The righteous one, on the other hand, resembles the sun. You will always find him serene, no matter what happens. He unites his contentment to the divine life and, from then on, he enjoys a peace which nothing can trouble. The angels told the shepherds on earth: "Peace to men of good will." Who among us does not know these words? Yet who are the "men of good will" if not those whose will is always united to the will of God and who consider this will of God as good and perfect?" We have not always understood this meaning which Saint Alphonse brings out from the words "men of good will. The man of "good will" is simply the man whose will always intermingles with the will of God, the latter being neither more nor less than that which occurs here and now.

The idea of "submission" to the will of God is therefore directly linked to the idea of peace. One day the companion of my travels in Afghanistan, Mohamed Ali Rahonaq, spoke to us on the theme: What is Islam? He began in this way: "Islam is made up of two words; the word "Islam" itself which means "submission" and the second which is "salaam" which translates as "peace be with you." Islam is therefore peace through submission." How could the one whose will intermingles with the divine will to the point of being able to say like the Hindu swami, "my will is done," not live in peace? Saint Alphonse also tells us: "He who lives in continual union with the divine will possesses perfect and continual joy." He then quotes from the Book of Job: "Who has resisted God and remained in peace?" And he brings us closer to the acceptance of the unacceptable and incomprehensible. "And when adversities happen to us, let us accept them without exception from the divine hand, not only with patience but with cheerfulness...If you aspire, here below, to know true joy, always and in everything unite yourself to the divine will...Say: yes, Father, may it be because it has pleased you that it be...God governs our life for our advantage and better than we could ever do it or desire it ourselves. He must wish for each thing as it is." I could offer many more quotes.

If we enter into the detail of these little works, they systematically evoke all the aspects of our existence, health and illness, wealth and poverty, friendship and betrayal, and also -- for there is great depth in these simple texts -- our inner states. It is the will of God that, today, I am agitated during meditation. It is the will of God that in this moment that my heart is dry, that I am without love, that I do not feel grace at work within me. There are times when, after the heart has been vibrant, ardent, immersed in beatitude, sterility returns once again. The Christian spiritual masters have always insisted on acceptance without regret or reticence of these difficult moments, but always through fusing our will with the divine will, which is the foundation of the practice.

For example, the fact that a monk cannot be at mass because he is sick must not make him suffer. Not only has this monk no right to complain, but he must see that it is much more beneficial for him to accept being unable to attend mass than to go if his health had permitted it. And for those who are not engaged on the Christian mystic and ascetic way but who aspire to a spiritual life and are animated by an intense search for depth and transcendence, this perfect adherence, here and now, of our will with the divine will takes on the shape of acceptance, here and now, of all our inner difficulties and of our emotions of the moment even if these emotions originate in the fundamental sin: refusal.

ACCEPTANCE IS NOT RESIGNATION

Here a danger appears: a pretended acceptance of the divine will can become the excuse and justification for our laziness. I accept not only the external events but I also accept the vicissitudes of my inner life, here and now. Yet, to say "yes, I am like this, I submit myself, I incline myself, it is the will of God," carries a trap: no more effort to change, no more effort to progress. Certainly, I choose with all my heart these inner troubles, I choose with all my heart this incapacity that I feel this morning to meditate, but this is not an excuse to settle into it, to justify myself in remaining in that state. Too often, the "lyer" as Christ said, very ably takes hold of this "non-duality" to compromise our asceticism in order to maintain us in lack of accomplishment, to keep us from the efforts and progress which are possible for us. Obviously, if we seek perfection in dreams of becoming the perfect man, we will never achieve it.

None of us will be the handsomest, the most intelligent, the funniest, the most brilliant, the most efficient. We must first understand this perfection as a blossoming of that which we carry within us, a perfection in the sense of completion. We are in process of evolution: a small seed transforms itself into a tree so vast that all the birds of the sky come to make their nests in it. But the intellect has an utterly treacherous skill to slow down this progression, to justify our weaknesses, by presenting that which is either laziness or cowardliness as submission to the will of God. This is true in relation to our inner states and the level we have reached on the way. And it is also true for that which is asked of us by the different functions of our existence. For example, if as a father, my past errors have contributed to the fact that my twenty year old son is neurotic, unhappy and unsettled, it is obviously a magnificent excuse, not in relation to the past (which was what it was) but in terms of the present, to not do what is asked of me as a father.

I have no other will than the will of God; it is the will of God that my son is unsettled and miserable; God does everything for the good of my son: I submit myself to it! Consequently, I do not play my role as father, I do not attempt all that is possible to help my son recover from his suffering and to find happiness. There is then a double danger: in relation to our own inner transformation and our evolution on the way, and in relation to our possibilities of action. Here there intervenes the other side of what we call "the acceptance of the will of God" or the "fusion with the will of God." What does God ask of me? How will I be the instrument of a wisdom vaster than my egocentrism, my desires, my fears, my humiliations?

This is not a matter of knowing if reality hurts nor of knowing whether it will humiliate my pride, but of knowing what is possible for me today. This is an important theme. We can express it by clearly distinguishing between "submission or acceptance" and "resignation." In resignation there is an aspect of dejection, defeat, and irresponsibility. The fusion of our will with the will of God has two faces.

The first is the yes to that which is. The second is: now, what is the response to give to this situation and how can this response avoid being the expression of my emotion, my subconscious, my opinions, my projections and be the expression of the will of God for whom I become an instrument. It is essential to understand with this second aspect, which is the "doing of the will of God through action," that it can only be the result of the first aspect which is "seeing the will of God in a particular situation." For those who have a desire to understand and use all the possibilities of their intelligence, there is an abundance of knowledge in the initiatory and esoteric teachings which we do not find in the simplicity of these little manuals of the inner life. And yet the simplicity of this attitude, if it is truly lived, if it includes the acceptance of the unacceptable and incomprehensible with inner certainty, can lead to the supreme Knowledge because it questions all our mental or intellectual limits, our prejudices, or value judgments.

We have each built our own idea of the world. Each lives in his own universe containing an ensemble of opinions and in which things are identified as good or bad, expectations are imposed on other people, this pleases me and that doesn't. Since the Tower of Babel, people live in their own world. Each only speaks his language. There is no true understanding. And yet this simple way can lead to Knowledge because it destroys "our" world. Our false and limited egotistic vision is turned upside down. This is not resignation, cowardice, nor laziness. This is reconciliation with life, and offers us the possibility of being happy and finding peace here below. That is why Durckheim tells us: "When you meet what is beyond all possibility of understanding and acceptance, the absolute unacceptable, will you be ready and convinced enough to choose the madness which is the supreme wisdom of saying yes? When the unacceptable, the unjust present themselves, remember: it is God Himself who comes to us, it is a benediction under the disguise of misfortune." With all my power of conviction as a Westerner of the twentieth century, I testify that this is true. The unacceptable, the incomprehensible is God Himself at work. If you can, without restriction, in a surge of faith and love, accept that which goes beyond your understanding, then you will find this peace which is rightly described as "passing all understanding."

BECOMING REAL

THE INNER CHRIST

by Jean-Baptiste Lotz

The theme of the inner Christ is well expressed in one of the maxims of Angelus Silesius: "Even if the Christ is born a thousand times in Bethlehem, If he is not born within you, You remain lost for eternity." The historical Christ is born in Bethelehem, the one who accompanies us from the outside, and we are fulfilled by following him. But it is in our being itself that is born the immanent Christ who, like a vital pulsation, animates us from our own depths. The inner and outer Christ are therefore indissolubly linked. Just as the outer Christ is useless to us without the inner one, so the inner one cannot subsist without the outer Christ.

In the light of this polarity and the tension it engenders, we shall compare the spiritual "Exercises" of Saint Ignacius of Loyola with Graf Durckheim's "initiatory therapy." The first exercises carry the mark of western Christian attitudes, while the second comes out of the eastern mindset, most especially from Japan. In the "Exercises," it is first the external Christ who imposes himself, but he carries the inner Christ and disposes us to receive him. On the other hand, "initiatory therapy" always leads toward the inner Christ, which does not exclude the exterior Christ and can prepare the way for him.

I. FROM THE EXTERIOR CHRIST TO THE INNER CHRIST

The "Exercises" give central importance to the contemplation of the reign of Christ. We find here the call of the eternal King to follow him to conquer the world with him. Faced with this solicitation, an awakened being cannot remain deaf. Moreover, he will feel himself ready to respond with total devotion. In order to accomplish this, he will have to transform the entire conduct of his life and configure it through great struggle to that of Christ. He will be satisfied with the food and drink which the Christ presents to him, he will endure with Him the fatigues of the day and will watch with Him at night. If it is the will of God, he will offer to take upon himself all poverty, all injustice, all ignonimity. In the service of Christ, we cannot content ourselves with a minimal commitment; we must give ourselves with complete generosity. Inner transformation is also linked to outer transformation since it is a matter of taming the urges of our senses and to struggle against love of self.

The contemplation of the life, passion, and resurrection of the Lord puts things in clearer focus. The path which he traveled upon the earth under the sign of the cross led him to sit in glory at the right hand of the eternal Father. Contemplations which lead us to choice and decision are central to the "Exercises." We become filled with Christ's feelings and are liberated from the requirements of the Adversary. Only those who overcome inertia and half-measures and are entirely firm in their decisions can be successful. In this context, we can classify people in three categories, then conceive of three degrees of humility through which we are led to go beyond our own will and to submit ourselves to the will of God. The Gospel offers us a paradoxical teaching on this issue which has fascinated Eastern masters: "He who finds his life will lose it, and he who loses his life for my sake will find it" (Mt 10:39).

The same understanding is presented to us in an image: "Unless a grain of wheat falls into the earth and dies, it remains alone; but if it dies, it bears much fruit" (John 12:23). To introduce death into life is the principal trait of the disciple of Christ, an attitude through which the external Christ comes to maturity in the Christ within. The way which is summarily traced here is not described according to rational considerations, but from inner experiences. Saint Ignatius mentions three kinds of decisions. The first relies on the direct inspiration of God who confers on us such a light and such certitude that we are submerged by it. The second begins from inner experiences which necessitate a discernment of spirits, for he who seeks is not free from illusion and that which must be destroyed often takes on the appearance of perfection.

The extent to which human experience taken in its globalism, and spiritual experience determine this transformation in Christ rises out of the preliminary considerations in the "Exercises" where it is said that it is not a matter of knowing many things but of being capable of feeling and tasting them internally. We must then carefully observe how the Spirit of God acts on our sensitivity through trials and feelings of abandonment, and what states they awaken within us. The aptitude to "taste" (gustus) is the best guide for the mind to attain the "fruits" (fructus) which we seek. To receive their benefits, the "Great Exercises" necessitate four weeks, four hours a day. The process brings to mind the words of John the Baptist: "I must decrease so that he may increase." My own being must be reduced to the extent that it is penetrated by Christ, so that He can transmute all things in Him, transfiguring and renewing us.

Therefore the external Christ progressively penetrates and absorbs the whole person, in such a way that it lets the inner Christ grow within us. The ultimate goal of this evolution is a person completely transformed in Christ whose whole being and life have become transparent to his true self.

II. FROM THE INNER CHRIST TO THE OUTER CHRIST

When the way developed by Durckheim is called "initiatory therapy", we must define these two terms precisely. It is first of all a therapy, that is, a method of healing sick persons, specifically persons who are sick in their souls. Secondly, this therapy is called "initiatory" because it deals with an entry into mystery. Little by little, this therapy was enlarged, for it has to do with leading people from the superficial levels of their being to their deeper levels, from the existential to the essential. This is not merely a theoretical teaching, but an initiation in that it is experiential and a putting to the test of things which are not accessible because they have to do with this mystery which we carry in the deepest part of ourselves as an original source which fertilizes our whole life, and without which it disintegrates and dissipates. A process of maturing is begun through which our self turned toward the external world, which dominates life, becomes permeable to our true being.

Our self relates to the world to which we belong and cannot be disconnected. It is through this self that our true self must break through in such a way that our life which is beyond the world can enter into the world. That is how we reach that which is essential within us, that is how Being communicates itself in each one of us. Man becomes himself and reaches maturity to the extent that his life rises from the depths of his Being. For that reason, it is essential for him to reach an experience of Being, or at least to feel one's being. We reach this through meditation which resonates in man each time that, through his conduct, he reaches the level of the Essential. We must be careful to differentiate between meditation on a specific object and meditation without an object, which is true meditation. Most of the time we meditate on an object, turning toward images in our mind. Meditation, on the contrary, is without object, without determined content, for Being situates itself beyond all other themes: the foundation of all things cannot become a thing among others.

When we take the historical or external Christ as an objective reality, we often easily pretend that by centering on Him, meditation loses its specificity. Graf Durckheim evolved a significant way out of this problem. He began with the Absolute, which he encountered as the great "It" and by which he was completely ravished. The great "You" was first inaccessible to him because, in the manner of Easterners, he held a representation of the "Person" which was too anthropomorphic and had therefore a tendency to assimilate it to an object. Little by little, however, he experienced the Christ as a powerful impulse in his depths; he surrendered himself to it and let it blossom within him. Its essence is equivalent to the ultimate depth of the true Self and is inherent in the intimate constitution of the human being.

We may ask ourselves if Graf Durckheim himself penetrated this depth. Clearly, he sought the inner path toward the Christ, that is, the path of experience, and more precisely the one of meditative experience as opposed to the path of faith. In this way he reached the inner Christ who does not necessarily coincide with the historical Christ of the Gospels. We might ask ourselves whether he reveals our original constitution or whether he is grafted onto us. C. G. Jung tells us that archetypes are to be understood as sediment of the historical destiny of humankind in such a way that Christ is a typical archetype. This meaning given to the inner Christ must be completed and deepened by discovering in what way he is the perfect archetype. He does not merely represent human destiny, but the intervention of God in human history. Because we have been created in the divine plan according to this event, we carry its imprint from the beginning as prefiguration. That is why every person is marked by it.

This is true even of those who do not encounter the Christ explicitly and do not consciously re-actualize the saving gestures of God. In this sense, the inner Christ is not an archetype among others but the one who infinitely surpasses them all. Meditative experience can plunge deeply into these depths which ultimately lead to Christ. Graf Durckheim was a Christian from childhood. The impact of his baptism seems to have been temporarily eclipsed for a time and replaced by the meditative experience; yet, over the years, it came back to the surface. In any case, the first breakthrough of the "great experience" which happened to him in Munich before his stay in Japan was determined not only by Chinese spiritual heritage, but also by the writings of Meister Eckhart.

Nevertheless, they did not provoke a complete return to Christianity, particularly with the influence of Zen Buddhism during his eight years in Japan. Yet the purpose of the center which Durckheim founded at Todtmoos-Rutte after his return from the Orient in collaboration with Maria Hippius, who later became his wife, was not to form Buddhists but to help those who came to him to live from their depths. Many Christians were led to maturity on a path which made use of exercises originating from the East but were appropriately developed for them. Grace in the Christian meaning of the term penetrates these two stages: it leads meditation to its perfection, making it a truly Christian event, and revealing that all meditation secretly leads to Christian meditation.

This was the heart of Graf Durckheim's struggle. This journey is seen especially in the lectures which he gave for years in Frankfurt. The title of a recent publication gathering them together hints at his development: The Path of Exercise -- A Gift of Grace. The exercises which proceed from our efforts reveal themselves as gifts and works of grace. This emphasis is placed on an issue which bears witness to the new degree of maturity which Graf Durckheim achieved. Grace always reveals itself as a power which lifts us into participation with the life of God. At the same time, the exterior or historical Christ, from whom we receive these gifts, manifests himself with growing clearness in the inner Christ. This grace was made available to us through his sacrificial death and resurrection.

Exercise has the effect of making our faith more transparent, linking us to Christ and opening us to blessings from above. The more this process evolves and deepens within us, the more meditation reveals its fundamentally Christian imprint. Many signs suggest that Graf Durckheim traveled such an evolution, especially in the last year and a half which preceded his death. In the magnificent church of Steingaden, Christian rites for the dead were publicly celebrated for him. As for what occurred at his bedside in his last days, only a few intimate friends were privileged to know. But it is clear that the crucified Christ accompanied him during his illness and through his death.

BECOMING REAL

THE PATH OF INITIATION AND THE MYSTICAL LIFE

by Jacques Breton

The "path of initiation" in the work of Graf Durckheim is often mentioned as a journey which every person must follow in order to become open to life. Durckheim loved to quote the passage from the Gospel of John: "I am the way, the truth, and the life," on which he commented: "The Christ, the inner master is the way which, through truth, leads to the Great Life." He describes the spiritual experience as a mystical experience, a numinous one. But are they identical experiences? In The Double Origin of Man, he distinguishes the initiatory way and the mystical way, but does so by uplifting their common points: both are based on the "experience of being." Are the ways similar? Is it possible to follow the path of initiation without reference to an absolute?

On the other hand, is the mystical life conceivable without being linked to the psychic and physical behavior of the individual? Does the path of "personalization" necessarily open onto the mystical life? So many questions. We will try to answer them by calling upon Durckheim's teaching and the experience which I gained at his side.

BECOMING REAL

THE PATH OF INITIATION

Graf Durckheim teaches that the path of initiation makes us move from the existential level to what he calls "essential being," and that this is the one "which opens the door of mystery." He seeks to reach our true "self" and transform us into witnesses of Being in the world. In other words, it is the way of realization through which we acquire our true personality and become ourselves. This is a path. The beginning point is named by Durckheim the "existential self." We know him well. We live him ceaselessly in daily life. We feel his limits, weaknesses, disorders, prejudices. He is assailed by all his personal problems of guilt, anxiety, fear, doubt, despair sometimes, and suffering.

Certainly, he is also a carrier of aspirations, hope, love, joys, but our subconscious makes us act in opposition to the way we would like to act. As Saint Paul said: "I do not understand my own actions. For I do not do what I want, but I do the very thing hate" (Rom 7:15). And if the inner man is faithful to his own reality, he discovers another law within which opposes him and makes him a prisoner. Faced with himself, his multiple imperfections, his failures, man questions himself. Who is he? What is Being? Does he truly exist in the face of evil, suffering and death?

THE MASKED MAN

Man does not come into the world in a state of perfection. On the physical and psychological levels, he must pass from a state of infancy to that of adolescence, then to maturity. He must also create his own personality to become what he is in the form of a seed. What gives man his greatness and constitutes his liberty is the possibility of creating himself; he is in process of genesis. His life progressively develops from primitive chaos. Since man is still ignorant of what he truly is, since he does not yet have the will to master himself, disorder will reign in his life and create many conflicts; man will especially be carried away by his prejudices, his emotions, his instincts and passions. Certainly at the beginning, it will be the role of his parents and educators to teach him how to live, to take shape, but with how many errors of all kinds! Very often, these persons are also far from having resolved their own problems; moreover, they will be tributaries of a social context which emphasizes knowledge over being.

It will be important that the child succeed in school in order to take his place in society, that he acquires diplomas; the rest is superfluous. Certainly, many parents are still worried and preoccupied by social and religious formation, but is it a true apprenticeship of life? Does it not impose itself from the exterior like a necessary framework, but without an effective opening onto ultimate Reality, which alone would allow them to live? The strongest shock which I experienced, during my formation at Rutte, was becoming conscious of this fact. When I arrived, I thought of myself as a good Christian, a good priest, a religious man; yet, after three months, everything fell apart, as though everything I had learned was only plaster, a superstructure; the formation I had received was not integrated. Without realizing it, I played a role: that of a priest. Of course, one cannot deny this necessity.

To exist before others, man must at the beginning create this mask, this "persona," which hides all his miseries, his weaknesses and his inner fragilities and which allows him to be recognized. But very quickly he becomes its prisoner; it gives him the impression of living, but he lives in illusion.

FROM THE PERSONA TO THE PERSONALITY

How will man rise out of this state to live that which he is? Is the participation of Being necessary to live this path? To the extent that we understand the goal of the path as the full realization of who we are, we do not see how we can open ourselves to fullness without opening ourselves to the Great Life. How do we leave the relative without the presence of the Absolute? Is it not absurd to want to build a fireplace without fire to light it? Many of our contemporaries develop the external side of themselves: the faculties, the know-how, the senses, the body, without opening themselves to this inner fire, symbol of the Great Life. In my first meeting with Graf Durckheim at Rutte, he asked me to meditate on "I am." What upheaval those two words caused in my life!

Until then they were, for me, reserved exclusively for Christ; only Christ could affirm his divinity and declare "I am." It seemed blasphemous to pronounce them. Yet the true reason was that God remained exterior to me. Certainly I believed in His existence as an absolute, but He was only an object of veneration or moral order and not a true principal of life. In reality, I did not permit myself to exist. God alone had the right to be and I could only sacrifice myself like a slave before his master. This is what I told myself, but it was my psychological problems which were the cause of this attitude. Because of a very difficult childhood, I did not allow myself to be and I projected on God all my problems by living humility as an escape, an annihilation. But my immersing myself with these two words "I am," I felt that at each moment, in the depths of myself, I was only through the One who made me be. In this way, Graf Durckheim brought me onto the path of initiation with the yearning to follow it to the end.

BEING STRIPPED

At this stage, a real struggle takes place in us against the forces of opposition, the fears and anxieties which assail us. Are we not the most fragile creatures on earth? We cannot face life without solid protection, both exterior and interior. That is why we must build a whole network of securities and defenses. We create a shell which closes us in and keeps us from existing. A whole therapeutic work is necessary to become conscious of all these security systems and to let them go. By freeing ourselves from these inner defenses, these restrictions and taboos, do we not open ourselves to a great permissiveness, when even religion no longer plays its role of moral defense? That is why Graf Durckheim insisted on holding Zazen meditation every morning, even if we had been up late.

When everything is let go, it contributes to rediscovering a basis. When there is nothing left, it places us in the presence of our "essential Being," and becomes our cornerstone. Then a confidence is established, no longer in an external God, but in the One who, at the heart of our selves, gives us the daring to live, the strength to face and resolve our own problems. We are caught in our contradictions. Quite often, our education and social context emphasize one side of our being to the detriment of the other. If, for example, we live in a climate of gentleness, the other side, the "hard" one, will be repressed and will turn against us or brutally explode in anger. But we will face more essential oppositions, as though our whole nature was polarized. We are children of the earth but also children of heaven, we are attached to matter and animated by Spirit. We seek to unite earth and sky.

MAN AND WOMAN

One of the most difficult tasks will be to encounter within that which characterizes us the most: we are born sexual, man or woman, and we carry in our depths the other side of our nature. In this journey, we will have to develop and harmonize these two poles which are called in Taoism "yin" and "yang." In each of us there exists a masculine side which gives us the possibility of confronting reality to recreate it, and a feminine side which allows us to receive this same reality and open ourselves to it. Yet man, in relation to woman, will especially have a tendency to develop his "yang" side, that is, the strong physical side, the intellectual, scientific one, while woman will develop her "yin" side, the intuitive and receptive one. But a "yang" which is not rooted in "yin" is often negative and develops a powerful "ego." The other side can also occur, and this was my case. Having lost my father, brought up by women, with no men to deal with, it was my feminine side which developed.

My religious education only reinforced this tendency: charity consisted, first of all, in being reconciling with everyone. During my journey at Rutte, an important dream led me to a fundamental discovery. I dreamt that I was in an immense court room full of people. I was the judge; the condemned man was Hitler. When a therapist at Rutte asked me to play Hitler, it seemed impossible to me. I became painfully conscious of the fact that Hitler represented the will to power that I had crushed within myself. From time to time, this manifested itself through moments of anger or aggressiveness and, in a deeper way, inhibited my creativity. How could I assume this "yang" which frightened me, without being carried away by this current of violence? Without the power of this love, this extraordinary strength which comes to us from the One who is everything and who is also love, how can we recover our unity? Without this dynamism of unification which comes to us from the depths, I do not see how we can reunite our two poles which are in such opposition in our personality. How do we balance the forces of "yin" and "yang" and resolve our conflicts?

DYING IN ORDER TO LIVE

But we must resolve an even more fundamental conflict. Called to live, and to live in fullness, we find ourselves endlessly confronted with suffering, isolation, meaninglessness, death, painful situations and dramatic events. We often seek to escape by every possible means, and the fear of suffering is an enormous obstacle on our path. For example, how many persons, having undergone ruptures in their friendships, refuse for a long time to enter into a relationship which might help them to come out of themselves? Yet, it is impossible for us to face this immense problem if, in our depths, we do not yearn with our whole heart for life and all that comes with it: joy, happiness, peace, love. There is a "yes" that must be said again and again to this life which is communicated to us from within.

Is not the Being within us the source of this life? This is the fundamental choice which we will always have to make, as God teaches us in the great book of wisdom in the Bible known as Deuteronomy: "I call heaven and earth to witness against you this day, that I have set before you life and death, blessing and curse; therefore choose life, that you and your descendants may live, loving the Lord your God, obeying his voice, and cleaving to him" (Deut. 30:19-20). And it is this thirst for life which will keep us from fleeing or closing ourselves in our suffering. This suffering will have many causes: separation, failure, injustice. It will always be the sign of a journey to be undertaken or of a detachment to be accomplished, of an openness to be lived. Suffering is revelatory of a state which must change and it is useless and even dangerous to question ourselves too much over the causes.

The intellect risks maintaining this state, even reinforcing it. Yet, it is critical to receive suffering into oneself, so that it can progressively tell us what it represents for us; in any case, it will ultimately be the sign of a death, a death to be lived. Death is an integral part of life and no one can escape it. It will always present itself under the aspect of a rupture or an opening, the sign of a gift for a rebirth. The path is not continuous. In fact, we are caught in the mud of our psychic, mental and physical habits which hinder the intuition of the truth of Life. This intuition gives us the thirst for an immediate and total fulfillment. But our conditioning is a rigid obstacle to the suppleness of necessary surrender. That is why we go through indispensable stages which will engender circumstances, relationships, religious or ethical phenomena which correspond to our current state. Next to the great stages with which we are familiar, those of childhood, adolescence and maturity, there are many subtler ones to cross over.

There are so many barricades, fears and attachments within us! It is this crossing over which will present so many difficulties. For we must live these passages at the right time: if we delay, we will close ourselves in a kind of prison which keeps us from advancing; if we bypass the stages, we are then obligated to go backwards which is very painful. These passages can be provoked by circumstances, but it often happens that we choose them. For example, I decide to leave my professional position. I will then have to abandon a past with its positive aspects and I feel this as a death. Only the "inner Spirit" can let us know the value of this rupture. We are not masters of the future. We can only live the present and these choices affect the future. It is the One who is master of the future who must enlighten us. In our depths, this light will appear to us under the form of intuition to which we will have to answer yes or no. Yet these intuitions can also come from our subconscious or from what Saint Ignatius of Loyola calls a "bad spirit." We will have to learn to discern that which emanates from the Spirit.

At the beginning, the help of a spiritual master is virtually indispensable. Death can also have another meaning. Advancing on the path presents itself as a continual overture. From a very limited life in time and space, we must reach a life of fullness. The opening of the heart does not occur without a rending. We must go through detachments in order to re-establish more genuine relationships and move from an overly dependent state to a deeper one. Death is the possibility of giving oneself, and Being is essentially the One who gives Himself. If we are to receive life within us in order to exist, we can only receive it if we surrender ourselves completely to this inner source. We must live love. But divine love is a gift. Death within us, like exhalation which represents it, is the gift of ourselves which we offer to the One who is everything in order to unify ourselves to him. We can therefore say that the "Great Life" is beyond death and life because it unifies in us these two great attitudes of Being which are gift and receptivity. Finally, the path of initiation opens us to our true nature and to what we are.

It allows us to recover our unity, a harmony with others and with the world. On the spiritual plane, it makes us completely available for what we have to live. It helps us to receive that which is. We are entirely present. By transcending our emotions, we react with deeper affectivity. We are guided by that wisdom which comes to us from within under the form of intuition, the fruit of experience and the light of the Spirit. It is no longer personal interest or the need for success which causes us to act but the desire to recreate a more harmonious world, to establish better relationships and, as Graf Durckheim says, to "bear witness to Being."

BECOMING REAL

THE MYSTICAL JOURNEY

We cannot conceive of the path of initiation without continual reference to Being. But can we say that it is a
mystical journey? The path of initiation deals with our
human and spiritual development. But what is the mystical life? It consists in a true communion with the
Absolute. We must certainly not confuse it with mystical
phenomena such as clairvoyance, stigmatas, levitation, or
visions. All these extraordinary phenomena break the
course of normal life. They are only physical and psychic
consequences of the mystical life. They can fool us and
be the fruit of our imagination or of our subconscious.
Some mystics can be very advanced on the way without
having been touched by these phenomena. The mystical
life is an entry into the divine mystery, a mystery which
every person carries within. The mystical life is not only
inwardness or deepening of the self, but openness to this
mystery which transcends us and which requires us to
come out of ourselves in order to enter into this Beyond
and participate in this ultimate Reality.

Every person yearns, by nature, for this divine union. We
are created for the Absolute which alone can fulfill us.
From this perspective, we can say that the path of initiation usually leads to the mystical life. But we must
distinguish between the mystical experience and the mystical life. The experience is a temporary manifestation of
this life. Being cannot make itself known or reveal itself
directly to our intelligence or our heart. It is, in Itself,
beyond, the Wholly Other, the Inaccessible, the Ineffable. Yet, it manifests its presence through certain touches
which, in an instant, transform our life. Durckheim calls
this the "experience of the numinous," in reference to
Rudolf Otto's book on the sacred. It is rare that, at one
time or another, we do not make this discovery of the
Absolute within ourselves. It is like a call, a basis for

faith. There is grave danger in entering upon the path of initiation without first having lived this experience. When everything falls apart on the ethical or religious level, this belonging to Being, which has been revealed in our depths, remains and sustains us.

THE ENTRY INTO THE MYSTICAL LIFE: VALUE AND WORTH OF THE HUMAN EFFORT

Entry into the mystical life cannot occur in a natural way. Being transcends our nature. To move from the relative to the absolute, from the limited to the infinite, from time to eternity, we must cross over a great abyss. It is an illusion to believe that, through our efforts and perseverance, technical means will be capable of opening us to this dimension. We can give ourselves the illusion of being God, but that is a permanent lie. The myths of original sin and the tower of Babel express very well this temptation. Yearning for this absolute of beauty, light, and power, we will try everything to attain it. But it is all in vain. Instead of opening ourselves up to truth, we often sink into darkness. In accord with all traditions and all mystical experience, we must affirm that it is Being alone that can, of Itself, make us cross over this abyss. It is Being which comes to unite itself with us. "It is not we who seek God, but God who seeks us," Durckheim wrote.

So what is our part in this process? Should we say, with some, that our effort is worth nothing and that everything depends on the divine will? This goes against all the experiences of the mystics. Without denying the assertion which states that everything comes from Being, our part remains crucial. If this were not the case, what would be the good of the path and the human efforts required to make the journey? It is necessary for us to prepare ourselves for this encounter. If we can do nothing without Being, divine Being can do nothing without us. If respect is the foundation of human relationships, it is because we are created in the image of the One who is Respect par excellence. There are three attitudes which will allow us to open ourselves to the mystical life: --faith --courage and availability --asceticism Faith is the first attitude.

How can I open myself to the beyond if I refuse to believe it in? We must be careful not to confuse faith with belief. The latter is only the expression of a desire for God, whose existence is proven to us from the outside. Faith is born from experience. But we must be able to recognize this experience as coming from Being. Many persons refuse to accept the possibility of this ultimate Reality in the face of suffering and evil. Among intellectuals or scientists, fashionable thought is the opposite of inner knowledge. Yet almost every person, as Graf Durckheim observed, has had this experience of the numinous. In a moment of their lives, they have been powerfully seized by some beauty or love which overwhelmed them. This experience comes to concretize what they may have discovered in books, both sacred and mystical. But this faith can fall into forgetfulness because we are too absorbed in our earthly occupations. It must be maintained continuously through prayer, meditation, the reading of the sacred word, listening to a master, the support of a community.

Faith must therefore be developed in order to become certainty, confidence, and knowledge of the divine within. Being will still remain inaccessible for a long time to our senses and to our intelligence. Only the divine Spirit can know Being. It will take a long time before my spirit can unite itself to the eternal Spirit and contemplate God face to face. Only certainty of this presence given to us through faith can lead us on the journey. The more we approach the divine fire, the more our faith will be enlightened, vivified. But beforehand we will go through many deserts and nights of purification. All our senses, our intelligence and our heart must be transformed in order to open themselves to this absolute. A typical, symbolic example is given to us in the exodus of the people of Israel under the guidance of Moses.

The path toward the Promised Land where they will live this covenant with God must go through the Red Sea. This symbolizes death and life. In this sea will be drowned the Egyptian army, a symbol of the dominating and conquering "ego." But thanks to divine intervention, it will let pass the people in quest of God. Then this people will cross the desert where they will linger for forty years before reaching the land of the Covenant. In their journey, they will be guided by a luminous cloud. The passage through water symbolizes this radical experience very well. There is no turning back. The individual definitively leaves a land, a family, a way of life where he is still slave to himself, to let the Spirit guide him. While still very dependent on a world where he was prisoner of his needs -- security, recognition, affection -- he enters into the spiritual adventure under the crook of a master.

But this adventure leads him through the desert or the emptiness and not directly to enlightenment. There the faith which was symbolized by the luminous cloud will be his only guide. This journey can last a long time. The second attitude is courage. Fear is the greatest obstacle that we encounter on the way. Fear of changing our way of life, our habits, our relationships, our way of thinking and seeing --while risking possible solitude-- but especially fear of the Absolute. This fear is justified. We read in the Old Testament: "Man cannot see God and live." The anguish of losing oneself in the Absolute will engender in us the anguish of becoming nothing, and finally, the fear of suffering. I will always remember this priest, the director of my seminary, who told us: "You know, I never asked to be a saint, because I knew too well what that would cost me." It is true that entry into the mystical life cannot occur without pain, without suffering.

As Saint John of the Cross wrote, we will have to go through many nights: night of the senses, night of the intelligence, and even night of faith. We will therefore need much inner strength, much love, to face all these trials. We will have to cross over a critical threshold. Our path inevitably leads us to a total impasse, an insurmountable obstacle, an inhuman suffering. We come upon the impossible. That is when we must "accept the unacceptable" as Graf Durckheim teaches, that is, we must place ourselves completely in the hand of God who alone can save us. A discipline, an asceticism, is indispensable. Asceticism is often confused with the practice of mortifications. But it is actually the way to "exercise ourselves to live who we are," as Saint Thomas said and Graf Durckheim took up.

This exercise requires a strong discipline in order to master ourselves, a nearly permanent control. Our nature is oriented toward the satisfaction of our senses, the thirst for pleasure and intellectual curiosity. How long does it takes us to acquire good habits and proper reflexes! I am certain that the method of Zazen and the correct practice of the so-called "martial arts," such as archery, are true apprenticeships to the mystical life. They require such a discipline of the body, such attention, such availability that, little by little, they put us in the service of that which is deepest within us. All the power which will animate the one who practices archery comes from within. It is called "ki." We receive it without calling upon our physical strength, but from our inner strength.

Is this not a way to make ourselves available to the deepest spiritual forces? But it can also open us to the most negative forces, especially since the mystical life, by removing all our securities, makes us vulnerable. Also, the more we advance on the path, the more we must exercise a great vigilance in order not to be caught by the powers of evil. In every moment, our attention must be maintained through prayer, meditation, so as to be entirely there in that which presents itself to us. Zen and the prayer of the heart can be excellent methods.

THE DEGREES OF THE MYSTICAL LIFE

It would be very difficult to compare the mystical experiences of different traditions. Language will always be imperfect to express them. These experiences remain inaccessible to our understanding. For example, in Japan the word "love" does not exist. When I asked a master how to become a better instrument of love, I did not understand his answer, but I was filled with such a powerful love that I was ready to give my life. The mystical life includes several degrees which appear under different forms in various traditions.

It is a path with no end, but which goes through stages. Saint Teresa of Avila spoke of seven castles of the soul and Saint John of the Cross referred to successive nights. For others there is the passage from being engaged to the mystical wedding. In Zen Buddhism, the mystical way is compared to the relationship between a man and his ox whom he tames little by little until he is one with him. We progressively enter into the divine mystery and feel our being as different from the Being we seek. The "self" becomes an obstacle to union with the Absolute. The "I" years to disappear so that divine Being can be everything within it. If it still says "I," it senses that its "I is God Himself," as Al Hallaj stated. This is the very mystery of the divine life which consumes the human being like fire to make us similar to Him.

According to the witness of Saint John of the Cross, we know that divine Being is in all things and that all things are in Him. And we know all things through God Himself and not God through the creatures. We discover that this Life and Being and harmony are God Himself in movement. "It sees in the wink of an eye what God is in himself and what he is in creatures," we read in Life, the flame of Love. It seems that He moves in us and we in Him. Undoubtedly, we will always have to awaken to this presence. This awakening is like a communication of the divine life in our own substance so that we become one with it.

THE MYSTICAL LIFE AND RELIGIOUS TRADITION

Nevertheless, we cannot enter in the mystic way without rooting ourselves in a religious tradition. The path to reach it is too difficult: "Narrow is the way which leads to the mystical life" (Rev. 3:20). Not only is the experience of those who have gone before us necessary, but so is the presence of a master, of an asceticism, a ritual, and a community. Moreover, the whole of religious history shows us that the mystical life does not arise spontaneously. It is based in the great current which travels through humanity since creation. This current will always be linked to a spiritual past. The Buddha, the one whom in history we call Siddharta, is connected to the Hindu current even if he separates himself from it. In the same way, Christ is the fruit of the whole Jewish tradition. All the Christian spiritualities (ignatian, franciscan, dominican, carmelite) found their inspiration in Jesus Christ.

This is an oral transmission which occurs from heart to heart, from master to disciple. We see appearing, in our era, a blossoming of systems, itineraries, psychological methods which call upon science, experience, and knowledge of human behavior. Many theories have appeared whose goal is to teach us to better know ourselves in the face of our problems and to help us to live better. Certain techniques relate to the individual in his totality, including the spiritual, but it is more subliminal than a direct experience to absolute Being. Graf Durckheim's value was to consider this relationship to Being as the foundation of all development of the personality.

It is true that it is tempting to draw only upon human methods to evolve. Even with the best intentions, we tend to reject all spiritual contribution as being external to our research of the moment, especially when our difficulties have often been aggravated by a poorly integrated religion, a religiosity which kept us from living. On the other hand, we find in religious traditions a rejection of all psychological methods in order to maintain the purity of the spiritual quest. And even in serious psychological cases, many persons have difficulty in calling upon a psychoanalyst or a psychiatrist. They have the impression that these psychologists interfere in intimate and sacred areas which belong only to God.

All intervention seems like a sacrilege or a lack of faith. "Isn't sin the reason for all our disappointments? And God alone can free us from it." Graf Durckheim's contribution is to show that the mystical life is essentially anchored in the wholeness of the human being. It is part of a reordering of man in his corporal, emotional, and mental dimensions, and makes this unity possible. Thanks to him, the mystical life is no longer reserved for an elite living in monasteries, but is offered to every person of good will.

BECOMING REAL

THE JOURNEY OF THE "NOBLE MAN": MEISTER ECKHART AND GRAF DURCKHEIM

by Jean-Yves Leloup

Graf Durckheim often spoke of Meister Eckhart as "his" master. His acquaintance with the great mystic goes back to the twenties when he experienced his first "break-through of Being": "Everything existed and nothing existed. Another Reality had broken through this world. I myself existed and did not exist...I was seized, enchanted, someplace else and yet here, happy and deprived of feeling, far away and at the same time deeply rooted in things. The reality which surrounded me was suddenly shaped by two poles: one which was the immediately visible and the other an invisible which was the essence of that which I was seeing. I truly saw Being..."

In German, we would say with Heidegger: "Das sein im Seienden: I saw being in that which Is." "It is not surprising that, in this context, Meister Eckhart created such an explosion within me. I could not put down his "Treatises and Sermons" which I perceived as an echo of the divine music I had just heard. I recognize in Eckhart my master, the master." When we reread the treatise of the "noble man," we can see similarities in thought and it would be interesting to read Durckheim as an echo of Meister Eckhart, who himself was an echo of the first tradition of Christianity and particularly of Origen. From echo to echo, we return to the creator Logos, to the silent song of the One whom Graf Durckheim and Meister Eckhart loved to call "Being."

THE DOUBLE ORIGIN OF HUMANITY

Eckhart tells us: "We must first know, and Revelation teaches it to us, that there is in man two natures: the body and the spirit. That is why it is said in Scripture: who knows himself knows all creatures; for all creatures are body or spirit. Therefore Scripture says in speaking of humanity that there is an external man and an inner man. The inner man is called a new man, a celestial man, a young man, a friend and a noble man. It is of him that our Lord is thinking when he says that a noble man left for a distant country in order to discover a kingdom and then returned." Graf Durckheim does not speak of the double nature of man, but of his double origin, celestial and earthly, and observes that the West has forgotten the first for the sake of the second. Existential man has suffocated essential man.

When Alphonse Goettmann asked him what the kernel of his teaching was, Durckheim answered: "It is taking seriously the double origin of human beings, the "celestial" one and the "earthly" one. The West has forgotten this in relegating the "celestial" one to the realm of faith and believing that only the "earthly" one can be the object of experience and practice. The West has frustrated persons in their spiritual development. Yet the celestial origin of humanity is our essential being, that which participates with Divine Being and can become conscious of It in specific experiences. We are citizens of two worlds: an "existential" one which is a conditioned reality, limited by time and space, and an "essential" one unconditioned and beyond time and space, accessible only to our inner consciousness and inaccessible to our powers. The destiny of man is to become the one who can bear witness to the transcendent Reality at the very heart of existence. To achieve this, we must first learn to take seriously the experiences through which, in privileged moments, Being touches us and calls to us. This is the fundamental meaning of all spiritual exercise as I understand it: to open ourselves to our essential being through experiences which manifest it and to enter upon a way of living which allows us to bear witness to Being in daily life."

Rather than speaking of two natures or of two origins, we could say: "the double polarity of man" to avoid a "dualist" interpretation. Matter and spirit, the essential and the existential have a single and same origin; the difficulty is not to oppose one to the other or to develop one aspect of the human being over the other. We must harmonize the inner and the outer, the essential and the existential, and rediscover our transparence. It is well said that the noble man "went into a strange land" (forgotten essential Being became "strange" for existential man) where he discovered a kingdom (the world inhabited by the presence of the Spirit is discovered as a kingdom.

It is no longer the self which reigns but Being itself and he returned to his home (in the terminology of Graf Durckheim, he returned to bear witness to Being in daily life). The important thing is this "going and returning" between heaven and earth, between the inner and the outer, the material and the spiritual. The fathers say that this is the appropriate work of "divinized man": the one who "does," who incarnates the love of God, "on the earth as in heaven." But before we can enlighten the earth we must rediscover our sky, that space, that infinity, that place where the Son is born within us.

THE INNER CHRIST

Graf Durckheim often spoke of the Self of man or of his essential Being as the "inner Christ": "We must understand that life has meaning only through bearing witness to essence, to the whole of life which is the Word, the inner Christ, the universal Christ present in each one of us, in all things." "The essential Being is the absolute within man, the source of his freedom where the Divine expresses Itself through an individual and particular form in the world of space and time. Each man should be able to say with Saint Paul: "It is no longer I who live, but Christ who lives in me"; for the experience of essential Being is the experience of Christ present within us, and the unity which is accomplished in that moment must be felt like that of "the vine and its branches." "When Christ said: "No one comes to the Father but by me," the Christian gives it an easy intellectual meaning based on concepts, objectifying it and seeking Christ on the outside through who knows what sort of imagination.

While in reality Christ invites man to leave the horizon of his existential self, to plunge into his essential Being which is the Christ himself in order to encounter the Father with him and in him." But does to "dive into our essential Being" mean to find the Christ? Is it not an idealization of oneself? Narcissus crowning himself in the name of Christ? Inflation of the ego? Could we not reproach Durckheim with what Jung was accused of: "The Christ is not an image of the Self, it is the Self which is an image of Christ!" With Durckheim, it would seem that the Self or essential Being is in the image of Christ, Christ being for the Christian tradition the image and resemblance of God inscribed in each one of us.

All deep anthropology reveals itself to be a Christology (if we do not give to this word the limitation of a historical tradition but the revelation of the human-divine depth of man). In any case, this theme often developed by the Fathers (especially Gregory of Nyssa) was present in the writings of Meister Eckhart: "The noble man, the inner man, is the field where God, the One who Is, planted his image and resemblance and where he throws the good seed, the root of all wisdom, all art, all virtue, all goodness, the seed of divine nature. This seed is the Son of God, the Word of God." And Origen tells us: "Since it is God Himself who has sown this seed in us, we can cover it and hide it but never entirely destroy it nor extinguish it for it always burns and shines and always tends to rise toward God." Whether Christian or not, every person carries within a "divine seed" --he is a child of God-- and Eckhart insisted with Origen on the innate and inalienable character of this filiation. In saying this, he is only quoting Scripture: "The Word is the true light which enlightens EVERY person. . .The darkness cannot overcome it" (prologue of the Gospel of John).

If we cannot destroy our essence, we can nevertheless forget it, and that is the human drama, the cause of our anguish. Graf Durckheim often takes up this theme: the repression of essential being is, even more than sexual and creative repression, the cause of our suffering and worry. Yet God seeks us and if we could clean the cup, the living waters would surge forth. Eckhart writes: "Concerning the inner man, the noble man, in whom is imprinted the image of God and sown the seed of God, the great master Origen tells us in a parable how we become conscious of this seed and this image of the divine nature and essence which are the son of God himself: the Son of God is in the depths of the soul like a source of vivifying water. When we throw dirt in it, that is, earthly desires, it is covered over and hidden to the extent that we no longer recognize or find it. But in itself, it remains active; as soon as we take away the earth which covers its surface, it reappears and we see it again. Origen says that this truth is found in the first book of Moses, where it is written that Abraham had dug wells of living water in his field, but that evil people had filled them with dirt; but when the earth was removed, the sources became active again."

BECOMING REAL

The Christ is not a model to imitate from the outside, for we could only be caricatures. He is the principle of life. To be united to this principle is to be united to others through the "essential"; we then find ourselves to be brothers and sisters, not sentimentally but ontologically. "There is only one essence, and I believe that, as soon as the spiritual or transcendent eye opens within us, we can see in the other what we are in our essence. Then there is a true encounter between two beings rooted in their essential being, an encounter of essence to essence, an encounter with the Christ."

DETACHMENT AND LETTING GO

To reach this union of heaven and earth and this Awakening to the Man-God within, Graf Durckheim along with Meister Eckhart proposes two great ways: "letting go" and the "acceptance of the unacceptable." Letting go in the language of Meister Eckhart and of the Christian tradition is called "detachment": "I read many writings from both pagan masters and prophets, from the Old and New Testaments, and I have sought seriously and with great zeal for that which is the highest and finest virtue through which man can best unite with God and become through grace what God is by nature. And when I penetrate all these writings as much as my reason can, I find only this: pure detachment is above all things."

Detachment is not disdain or indifference but freedom in relation to what we possess and to what possesses us, freedom from those unconscious "imprints" which are the source of our attachments. Graf Durckheim speaks of it as letting go: "Letting go implies and requires the renunciation of guaranties. Essential confidence can only grow to the extent that man dares to relentlessly renew his surrender of securities. This is the confidence which needs no proofs, a simple confidence trusting the unknown. This is the formula "die and become" which animates all living things. This primordial formula is also the fundamental law of the initiatory life. It implies renunciation endlessly renewed in favor of essential Being and the new life which it brings forth.

The blossoming of essential Being presupposes the annihilation of the profane self." Graf Durckheim almost quotes Meister Eckhart word for word here: "There where the self is God cannot enter. There where it no longer is God cannot not enter. Man must be stripped of all things and of all works, both internally and externally, so that he may be a proper place in which God can work." Letting go or detachment is therefore more than a simple moral attitude, but replaces an egocentric attitude with a theocentric one, implying an authentic "metanoia," an openness of created being toward uncreated Being; again we find this theme of the human being called to become God.

The law of this becoming is "annihilation-elevation" (kenosis-anastasis) described in the epistle to the Philippians: "Who, though in the form of God, did not count equality with God a thing to be grasped (he let go of that which he considered the substance of his being). Therefore God has highly exalted him (resurrected) and bestowed on him the name which is above every name ("I Am" the One who Is). You must know the truth: when the free spirit remains in true detachment, it constraints God to come toward his being and if he could remain formless, he would receive the very being of God."

LETTING BE -- ACCEPTING THE UNACCEPTABLE

In daily life, letting go as a way of being must go through the "acceptance of the unacceptable." We could perhaps translate these words as "non-duality with the inevitable." It is not a matter of resignation but of union, of saying yes to that which is. In his study on the different monastic orders, Thomas Merton observed: "The monk is the one who lives in the real, and his mission is to become so real, under the action of the Spirit of the One who is, that his own life is a pure 'amen,' a conscious echo which freely answers 'yes' to the infinite Reality of God." But it is not necessary to be a monk or a mystic to be able to say this "yes."

We only need to be in good health. In his book "The Gestalt Therapy Book," Joel Latner writes: "Health does not equal happiness or success. It is a matter of being one with the circumstances where one finds oneself. Even death is a healthy event if we become one with our present reality, whatever it may be." These various quotes remind us of the universal value of the teachings of Graf Durckheim on this subject: "Acceptance is the key which opens the door to Life... In absolute weakness, when we can do nothing more, when we are abandoned to death, at that moment we can suddenly feel invaded by a great power in the very depths of our weakness. The power of the existential self based on what we have, what we know, what we can do is broken, and finally gives way to what we are in the depth of our essence." "It is precisely at the very moment when you are separated from that which is dear to you and accept the unacceptable, that a divine Love can invade you and give you shelter.

Then, in the midst of sadness and isolation, you are suddenly filled with joy and peace." "To accept is to "live one's death!" Throughout one's life there are little deaths that must be accepted and "letting go" progressively becomes second nature. To avoid it and fight suffering is natural, but when it comes, we must accept it to receive what is beyond it." Graf Durckheim speaks of a Father Gregoire, an orthodox hermit who lived near Paris. "He had painted a magnificent icon representing Christ embracing Adam in hell. I asked him: "Father, what does this icon mean to you?" And he answered me: "If man recognizes himself in his hell, that is, sees the Devil within him, his meanness, his darkness, his great uncleanness, and instead of pushing all that away he forgives it in love, then the divine can illuminate him...For me, this is Resurrection." Letting go is also to accept that which is intolerable within us, our inner enemy, our shadow. Durckheim, as did Jung, reminds us that there is no rising toward the light without the acceptance of and the journey through our shadow.

We are not as we "should" be, we are as we are and it is as such that we must change and evolve. Graf Durckheim, like Meister Eckhart, seems a bit "gnostic" on this subject, in that evil itself can be approached in a non-negative fashion: it is through error that we find truth, it is by falling that we discover the miracle of standing. "Everything works for good for those who love God," said Saint Paul, "even sin" added Saint Augustine. The person on the path sees suffering and the inevitable as a way to reach his goal: union with essential being. It is not a matter of looking for suffering, but when it is there, we are to make it an "opportunity" for higher consciousness. There are places within us which do not exist as long as suffering and love have not penetrated them. While everything is whirling in the cyclone, the center remains still. It is toward this "center of the cyclone" at the heart of man that Meister Eckhart and Graf Durckheim, in the tradition of the hesychast Fathers, lead us, affirming that we can taste in the midst of tribulations something which is no-thing: within and beyond suffering, meaninglessness and death.

That is what the Christ himself lived: "Christ could not place himself in any other place than where man hurts the most. He puts himself at the heart of the unacceptable. Not only does he freely accept death, but also the absurd: no one had understood his message and most had rejected it. Also, he did not defend himself before Pilate or Herod or even among his own; without a word, he accepts all humiliations. Finally he is also in virtually total isolation: his closest friends betray him and abandon him...So Christ did not come to take away this suffering created by the world, but to teach us to accept the unacceptable as he did! The cross will be taken away only from the one who has carried it..." Christianity is not an apology of suffering for it remains an evil, a scandal even and we must do everything to free the world of it. This is the attitude of Christ who healed the sick and exorcised demons.

Yet Christianity also affirms that even suffering and evil can be an opportunity for the appearance of the great consciousness and of the greatest love; it also affirms that it is not suffering, meaninglessness or death which will have the final word, for "Christ is Resurrected": Love is stronger than death.

PURITY OF HEART

When the thief asked Jesus on the cross, "Remember me in your Kingdom," Jesus answered: "This day you will be with me in Paradise." He did not say as we might have expected: "you will be with me in my Kingdom." What is this paradise? What state of being and of consciousness does it symbolize? The staretz Zozima in The Brothers Karamazov, a typical witness of the Greek and Russian Churches, said: "We do not understand that life is paradise, for we only need to wish to understand it and suddenly paradise will appear before us in all its beauty." In other words: if our eyes were "open," paradise would be here. Paradise is seeing things as they are, but in order to see "that which is" how many filters must we see through? How many images, memories, fears and desires must we go through to join the Real as it Is?

For the Fathers of the desert and particularly for Cassian, the goal of the Christian life is "purity of heart" which allows us to see the One who Is in all that is. Asceticism is above all a clearing away, a vigilance before the essential. Meister Eckhart spoke of "poverty"; purity of heart and "poverty of spirit" are synonymous for him. "A man is poor when he wants nothing, knows nothing, has nothing...If man must truly be poor he must be as emptied of his created will as he was when he was not. I tell you this eternal truth: as long as you have the will to accomplish the will of God and desire the eternity of God, you are not poor, for he alone is poor who wants nothing and desires nothing."

This state of not-wanting and non-desire is the necessary condition for the manifestation of fullness -- it is the state of innocence or "paradise": to be without the "I" being -- to see things without "ego," without projecting our memories, that is the paradisic vision according to Meister Eckhart, a vision which brings us closer to another "I" which is no longer the "little self" but essential Being, the "I Am," the Principle of all beings.

Graf Durckheim joins with this insight when he calls upon us to go beyond learned beliefs to a lived faith: "When we see how many Christians identify themselves with this belief...in particular the religious orders! They have a feeling of guilt, and are afraid of being condemned to who knows what if they take the liberty of letting go once and for all of the huge weight of formulations learned since their youth and have confidence in the inner voice they hear within. I received a letter the other day from a older sister superior who wrote: "I am happy to have finally found within me the permission to seek out the divine reality which inhabits me and to find that bit by bit the plaster is falling!" What is this plaster if not a belief dictated by the Church?" We must therefore venture into the desert, which the Rhineland mystics called "necessary nudity."

153

This non-obstruction of the spirit and of the heart puts us in a state of "vacancy" which makes us "mothers of God" for, as Eckhart says with Origen, "we must become virgin in order to be mother." It is only in silence and innocence of the heart, poor and virginal of all thought, of all desire, that the Word can be born. Graf Durckheim tells us: "To create emptiness within oneself, to become a virginal cup, is a vital condition for every Christian. The Word can become flesh in us, but if we are encumbered by the multiple, we cannot "receive it" as saint John says, "because there is no room in our inn." As long as our consciousness is not freed, we remain deaf and blind, with "eyes that do not see, and ears that do not hear." The representations and mental images of God make of Him an abstraction and we must be rid of them to go from death to life."

Meister Eckhart compares us to a window through which shines the light of God. If the window is clean (virgin), it is completely transparent and cannot be seen at all. It is "empty" and we only see the light. But if we carry within us the stains of attachment and preoccupation, even spiritual ones, and then the window is seen because of these stains. To be rid of stains, fixations, all mental or psychic dust which keeps the light of the Spirit from manifesting itself in us, is the work and exercise suggested by the ancient monks when they speak of the "purity of the heart which allows us to see God," not as we imagine or conceptualize Him, but such as He Is. Saint John of the Cross, following in the footsteps of Meister Eckhart, stated that "to love" is to work at releasing oneself and stripping oneself from all that is not God (to strip oneself of all that is not real for the love of Reality).

But Cassian reminds us that purity of heart is not the ultimate goal. Among the ancients, paradise is not the sky, rediscovered innocence is not yet the Kingdom, emptiness is only the condition for the light to manifest itself. Though the window may be clean, that is not what makes the sun shine. The spirit can be perfectly pure and empty and yet the clarity of Awakening may not manifest itself. It is not because we raise the sails that the wind blows. The synergy of effort and of grace are the two wings which the bird needs to fly. Paradise is our affair, but the Kingdom comes when the Wholly Other, another Consciousness --infinite, uncreated, immutable -- lives in this paradise of the heart when it is noble, purified and open. In summary, the journey of the noble man according to Eckhart and Durckheim can be stated as follows:

1. Becoming conscious of our polarity, earthly and celestial.

2. Deepening this polarity leads to the apprehension of the inner Christ and the theandric structure of humanity "truly human - truly divine."

3. The forgetfulness of this divine polarity is the cause of the shadow and human anxiety. Through detachment and letting go, we can find "well-being," that is, a life lived in the Presence of essential Being.

4. Remaining near essential Being, the noble man will become able to experience the "non-duality of the inevitable" which will lead him through deaths and resurrections to Openness. This journey is the one of the ancient fathers, carriers of God, peaceful witnesses (hesychasts) of the light and of the eternal Love in the midst of the world.

BECOMING REAL

DURCKHEIM AND THE BIBLE

by Alphonse Goettmann

Since in the West the Bible is no longer understood in the light of the early tradition, we have lost the taste for its reading. We no longer know how to approach it: why read a text several thousand years old? People have more or less put it aside and do not understand its content. For they do not realize that they are not to seek knowledge from it but an encounter, not a reading but a transformation! The truth lives in the heart of the people: the Bible is a real presence, that of Christ; the Bible is the book of my transformation, where I become god! We can only approach the Bible experientially.

We do not enter it only with our intellect, but with our whole being. It is understood only if we fulfill it and it is of value only for the one who makes of it his or her path. It then offers a knowledge, which is to be born with Christ and reborn with Him on levels of consciousness which deepen endlessly. It is a becoming in wisdom and saintliness where the incessant encounter with Christ acts by osmosis and configures us to Him. Here I learn how I am born and why, the reason for my suffering and the great joy which is promised. I discover, beyond all its absurdities, that life has meaning, that I am loved with a mad love, that God has only one desire: offering Himself to me, here and now, in a liberating experience which transforms me from top to bottom and makes of me a new creature.

What does all this have to do with "reading"? If the Bible is a "real presence," it first comes to me as communion, inscribing itself in my anthropological structure and revealing my unknown mystery and my itinerary along with my unique vocation. But how can I accomplish this if I have no forerunner to show me the way? This is exactly the role of the tradition. The Fathers never studied the Bible at a distance, by interpreting and speculating on it, but their whole theology is a description of their experience which retraces in letters of fire that which occurs in their own being, when the text truly begins to live. That is why they are so utterly molded by the Bible and only think, speak and live through it. They have assimilated the Bible and the Bible has assimilated them.

This is where we find Graf Durckheim's source. Not that he had a special knowledge of the Bible, although he was never separated from the Gospel of John which he loved deeply; nor did he have a knowledge of the Fathers though he never ceased to repeat: "My source is master Eckhart...I always return to his "Treaties and Sermons"...I recognize in Eckhart the master, my master" (from Dialogue on the Path of Initiation). This placed him directly in line with the tradition. Eckhart represented, in his time (thirteenth century), a strong reaction to the theology of the schools which was abstract and lifeless. He turned to the ancient ones: Saint Denys the Areopagite, Gregory of Nyssa and many others belonging to that line of mystical "apophatic" theology which says nothing of God without having experienced it. For them, every concept of God is a sham, an idol.

The least thought of God keeps us from meeting Him! We must exclude all rational activity and can only unite ourselves to God by transcending our intellect. In other words, the experience to which Durckheim invites us in every sentence of his many writings is a way of approaching the Bible, of understanding it inwardly and corporally as will be seen shortly. In this effort he is a pioneer at the turning point of history. Beyond the fog which separates us from this great tradition, Durckheim was able to recover the lost thread, due to his own experience, and restored it in the language of today. We present here only a few of his fundamental intuitions which are keys teaching us to live differently with the Bible. They illumine the Bible just as the Bible illumines them.

THE DOUBLE ORIGIN OF HUMANITY

After more than half a century of research and experience, at the end of his life Durckheim summarizes his position in the following manner: "If you asked me today to express in one sentence the kernel of my teaching, I would answer: taking seriously the double origin of humanity, celestial and earthly. The West has forgotten it: by believing that the celestial was the exclusive realm of faith and that only the earthly could be the object of experience and practice, the West has frustrated man in his spiritual development.

Yet, the celestial origin of humanity is part of his essential being. In the depths of our being, we human beings participate with divine Being and can become conscious of it in particular experiences. It is the experience of an unconditioned reality opposed to the conditioned reality of the existential self and its world. We are citizens of two worlds: the one of existential reality, limited by time and space, accessible to reason and its powers, and the one of essential reality, which is beyond time and space, accessible only to our inner consciousness and inaccessible to our rational powers.

Our destiny is to become such that we can bear witness to transcendent Reality at the very heart of existence." In these few sentences, we find a clear grasp of the strongest convictions of the ancient Christian tradition. They are an extraordinary light on the very first pages of the Bible and allow us to penetrate them through experience. "God created Man, man and woman he created them" (Genesis 1:27). As always in the Bible, there is a literal, historical or external understanding, and then the actual understanding which is inner and reveals us to ourselves. Durckheim offers us the key for this latter approach. "Man and Woman" is the double origin of human beings and at the same time the program for our existence. Our destiny is to perform the masculine work of penetrating the different fields of consciousness and attaining unity with the feminine within.

It is a matter of discovering the divine core in our depths and uniting with it. This unity in diversity is the "image of God" which is a unique God in Three Persons; and this image, according to the same text, must "become resemblance," that is to say, it must be carried into the fullness of its realization. This is the whole path of humanity. It consists in a nuptial attitude of loving attention which is the permanent background out of which arise all the Biblical texts from beginning to end. "Hear, O Israel!" That is why Durckheim could say that hearing was the most used of the senses on the spiritual path. From our creation we are "placed in the Garden of Eden" (Genesis 2:8), which, according to the Fathers, means precisely depth, interiority. And we then see all those great couples who, happy and tragic, describe us so well as they follow the path. Adam and Eve are therefore Humanity in its double origin of earthly ("Adama":earth) and the mystery of our celestial fulfillment to which we are called by the presence of Eve within us, to whom he awakens after a long sleep (Gn 2:21).

In duality, we become one through listening. That is exactly what Adam and Eve do not do: they eat of the tree of knowledge. Without considering the injunction of God who is listening, we live as though God did not exist and, instead of a path of fulfillment, we lose ourselves in external erring. We wed other gods outside of Him, feed ourselves with substitutes and forget our own essential depth which alone holds the secret and origin of humanity. That is why breaking with this reality can be called "original sin." It is the only one which each of us commits every day, and all our other sins are only symptoms of the first one. The word "sin" in Hebrew means: to miss the mark, to miss the meaning. There is no moral connotation: the man who has left the axis of his spiritual connection falls in an erring which leads to nothing but meaninglessness and absurdity. This is what we find with the following Biblical couple: Cain and Abel. Abel is guardian of the flocks, that is our existential dimension and the animals are our earthly, physical or psychic energies.

As for Cain, he is a laborer who should be working on his inner earth, the dimension of transcendence unconditioned by humanity. Thrown out, cut off from his roots, he goes off to build the temple on the exterior: cities, cultures, civilizations...As he is not seeking the Absolute in his depths, he goes to seek him on the outside, in the relative, and the latter can never respond to his waiting. So this man will ravage the realities of this world through idolatry and hatred, and he ends up reject them all. This is the case of the murder of Abel by Cain and the feeling of the nothingness of a world without God (Gn 4). All civilizations are founded on murder, the sweat of the brow, tears, blood...That which we wed outside of God dominates us and makes slaves of us. Esau and Jacob also represent our two natures. Esau is a hunter, a conqueror, the existential self. Jacob is the unconditioned being.

He takes the whole of the inheritance, that is, he receives all his energies, goes off into Laban, which symbolizes the inner path and seeks his feminine side to unite with her. It will take him two times seven years, double fullness, for this realization in Rachel. From their union will come the twelve tribes of Israel (Gn 25). These few examples which open the first pages of the Bible teach us to read the whole Bible in this way. This revelation of the mystery of humanity and its double origin is never a proposition of intellectual faith but an experience of life and a daily practice.

THE TRINITY OF BEING

The fall of humanity brought on the unfortunate distresses around which gravitate all of Durckheim's work. They are three in number and are the common denominator of all other suffering:

* the fear of death: a stream cut off from its source ceases to exist, that is a law of nature. A man cut off from his divine core, from which he receives himself constantly, will inevitably head toward suffering and death, and his existence is marked by this profound anguish, for everything is hostile and threatening to him;

* the meaninglessness of life: man is created to nourish himself of God and to unite himself to Him. If he does not respond to this fundamental aspiration of his whole being, his life has no more meaning, everything is absurd, and he is never satisfied;

* solitude: man living without God finds himself alone. He identifies himself with his little self and enters into a

world of division: life becomes "me against the world." The hypertrophy of the mundane self makes true encounter difficult and solitude inevitable. Yet this triple distress represents for Durckheim a reality which expresses the whole Bible. Man "in the image of God" is promised from the beginning a triple blessing: delighting in the life of God, possessing the Kingdom of heaven and powers through the gifts of the Spirit. Is it then surprising that Satan tempts Adam and Eve in their very happiness? Indeed, there are three temptations and they contain all the others (see Genesis 3):

* Adam eats of the tree of knowledge prohibited by God: he falls therefore into the world of enjoyment without God. But this enjoyment leads straight to death! Freud and his descendants have shown that "man dug his ditch with his teeth" and that the bed of Eros was in reality a tomb. Adam is then chased out of paradise, that is, he loses his interiority since he seeks his pleasure elsewhere, on the outside;

* "The tree was desirable" continues the text of Genesis, and this is the world of possession without God. We place our desire for infinity into the finite, in that which is mined by erosion and ruin. The richest man in the world is also the saddest man in the world. His golden palace is a prison whose windows open onto the absurdity of life and its meaninglessness. The text shows this in a realistic way: "The soil (possessions) is cursed...it produces thorns and thistles...sweat upon the face"; "You will be as gods," Satan promises.

This is the promise of the will to power of all the towers of Babel, great and small, where the confusion of tongues means incommunicability and infernal solitude; whoever has power dominates another but never encounters him. He is alone. This is made clear in the words: "Adam hid himself." Jesus Christ, the New Adam, comes to restore creation and lift humanity out of its fall. He is tempted by Satan in exactly the same way as the first Adam:

1. "Make bread from those stones": pleasure.

2. "Throw yourself from the Temple": power.

3. "All this I will give to you": possession. But the whole mission of the Messiah throughout the Gospel consists in healing the wounds of human beings opened by rupture and separation:

* faced with the anguish of death, He reveals the Source of all life: the Father;

* faced the despair of meaninglessness, He reveals the light of meaning: the Son who says: "I am the light...Whoso follows me does not walk in darkness";

* faced with the horror of solitude, He reveals the Holy Spirit who communicates the fire of Love. In other words: people in their triple distress are sick because of the absence of the Divine Trinity. We are created "in his image" and the path of our life is to reach "resemblance." When we experience being in our depths, it always manifests itself on the existential level as a force, a fullness in our weakness-death, like a Light in the darkness of meaninglessness and as Energy, Love, Movement at the very heart of solitude: Father-Son-Holy Spirit.

God comes to save us in our sickness and in saving us He recreates us in our Trinitarian dimension. Here we reach the summit of Graf Durckheim's metaphysical understanding. The theme of the "trinity of being" is the center of his thought. "Nothing exists outside of the Holy Trinity," he writes, "and each living being is an image of it. Everything comes from the Father to the Son, and from

the Son through the Holy Spirit it returns to the Father."
This is also the announcement prefigured in the Old Testament and its full revelation in the New Testament. This
is truly the culmination of the whole Bible and without it
we will never know this mystery. In all traditions, spiritual experience manifests itself under its triple aspect.
But it is only in the Christian tradition that this experience is revealed as three Persons. This is the
characteristic of Christianity as Durckheim so magnifi-
cently expressed it (see *Dialogue on the Path of
Initiation*).

THE LIBERATING EXPERIENCE

But how do we reach this fantastic experience? That is
the only question, conscious or unconscious, for a person
left to themselves. It underlies all that we do as the secret
engine of our initiatives. Durckheim replies: liberation
lives within each person as his deepest reality and this is
an incredible experience which everyone is called to
have as of now, and not only after our death. Everything
turns around this transforming experience whose fruits
are seen in the masters, but which is alive in us as well
under the form of a yearning, of something that we do
not yet know and which sighs in our depths while waiting to be discovered.

When Easterners have this experience, they call it "the
nature of Buddha" or "satori" enlightenment. We cannot
better describe the faith which is found in the Bible and
among the Fathers. Faith came into the West very slowly,
through the intellectual acceptance of external truths,
through beliefs which do not transform anyone. But this
is not the case in the primitive tradition. When Jesus
called his first disciples, he told them: "Come and see"
(John 1:39), which is an invitation to experience, and the
text adds: "They stayed with him on that day." Is this not
the most beautiful way to describe meditation? In any
case, the Christ never proposed a theory. A God who in-

carnates himself, who takes my flesh and blood, is to be experienced!

If the Christ is resurrected, the Living One par excellence, more real than all reality, his encounter can only be terribly concrete, far from any "belief." We should reread all of the Acts of the Apostles to realize to what extent the life of the first Christians was truly an experience of fire. Their daily lives had meaning only through this, their only motive for living was the resurrected Christ. They felt him present within and around them, and they only breathed through him! Joy was such that one could not mistake the authenticity of this life which triumphed everywhere. Even death was no longer an obstacle on their path as centuries of martyrs have testified.

Faith for the Christian was precisely this rigorous and existential experience of union with the Christ in his death in order to take part in his resurrection here and now. All that is said concerning this theme only makes sense if we can realize it ourselves, otherwise "the discourse is empty" (1 Timothy 6:20). Saint Paul insisted very strongly on rooting oneself in this experience, in particular in his first letter to the Corinthians. Next to rational and dialectical wisdom, there is the one which must be experienced and which transcends reason. Only this wisdom allows us to communicate with the living Christ within us and gives access to a completely new life, on the condition that we are liberated from subjection to verbal formulas and conceptual structures which are the "wisdom of language" (1 Co 1:17).

The experience that faith invites us to is the acceptance of a complete stripping, a letting go which means in reality "to be nailed on the cross with Christ," in such a way that the ego is no longer the principle of our deepest actions which henceforth proceed from the Christ who lives within us (Ga 2:19- 20). This is the center of life for the Christian and it opens onto a life of fullness. Faith is then no longer something added to our life, an unnecessary luxury, the belief in an external being which is added to our existence and with whom we entertain an alienating dependence: it is life itself in its essence, the Life of life, where it becomes plausible that without God there is no more person

This is a transcendence which is a "beyond at the heart of life" (Bonhoeffer) and that we can only reach, not through escape, but through "a deeper immersion into existence" (Kierkegaard). "For me to live is Christ" said Saint Paul (Ph 1:21), and each moment is therefore the best one to "let ourselves be seized by Him." Life itself is the way: "I am the Way, the Truth, and the Life."

This statement from Christ himself assures us that faith is not a doctrinal proposition to which we must adhere, but Someone whom we experience from moment to moment, if we would only live consciously in the present moment. This is a path of transformation which is never interrupted; it is a constant Easter with the Christ, the passage from death to Life. This is where we find the central message of Christianity, and Saint Paul and Saint John have no other theme in their Gospel. It is the first and last meaning of baptism which is the condition of the disciple. From the beginning, the baptized are called "the illumined ones" and their path is one of "initiation." But this illumination is not an unknown phenomenon, for it is Christ himself whom we experience.

The Christ identifies himself with illumination when he says: "I am the Light" (John 1:4-9), just as he identifies himself with the present moment when He says: "Before Abraham was, I Am" (John 8:58). He is the absolute present, that which IS, and those who do not live in this experience of faith are already dead: "If you do not believe that I Am, you will die in your sins" (John 8:24).

Durckheim often cited these texts during his conferences, for that is truly the key to his method. If God manifests Himself in the present, in that which IS, then to unite myself to the moment is to commune with God. Then comes the full and total acceptance of the present moment with all that it can contain, even the acceptance of the unacceptable, according to Graf Durckheim's great leitmotiv. This is Christ's fundamental attitude throughout his whole life, but especially seen in the moment of his passion. "There was only "yes" within him" said Saint Paul (2 Co 1:19) and it is this apprenticeship which he came to teach us, learning how to live in surrender and love: "Thy will be done."

This coming out of duality, where we become one with the event without the least resistance, is a true death of the ego, a crucifixion, for the purpose of a radically new way of daily living, a life of resurrection, a new style of life revealed by the Christ. This attitude is diametrically opposed to passivity or resignation; on the contrary, it engenders an action where the supernatural forces within us are liberated. Our whole depth is found in our power of receptivity which is our true maturity; then we commune with God, with other beings, with our own mystery and the secrets of creation. The person who lives in such a way has found peace and a "joy which no one can take away" (John 16:22).

THE WHEEL OF METAMORPHOSIS

The "wheel of metamorphosis," letting go--giving oneself-- surrendering--rebirth which structures the movement of the breath, is for Durckheim the concrete exercise on the path. It can be applied by everyone, without belonging to any tradition whatever. But the Christian, as he deepens the practice, discovers in the "wheel" a quasi "carnal" experiential reading of the Bible. "Letting go" is the first condition on the path, the first step without which there is no second. This commandment resonates throughout the Scriptures in a thousand ways, from "Go, leave your country" addressed to Abraham to the rich young man in the Gospel who is told by Jesus: "Go, sell all you have!" and the first beatitude which summarizes all the others: "Blessed are the poor!"

"To give oneself" needs no commentary as the gift of self is synonymous with love: the Bible was given to us only for this purpose, for it is the revelation of Love; every verse announces it or fulfills it without using the word, all the way to its completion where God reveals Himself as being Love in person.

To enter into this movement of the inner gift is to participate in the very life of the Trinity where all is gift from one Person to Another. "To surrender" is to consent to total abnegation, to death itself, and this placing of oneself into the hands of God, like "clay in the hands of the potter" as the prophet Jeremiah would say, is precisely the unconditional "yes" of which we have spoken, acceptance, even of the unacceptable. What is more unacceptable than death? This is the victory over all difficulty, great or small.

Here I am on the cross with Christ overcome, but it is also there and here only that can arise all life: "rebirth," inspiration. It is the kiss of the Creator upon his creature whom He never ceases to bring to life. In each of my inspirations is fulfilled that which is revealed from the beginning of the Bible: "God breathed into his nostrils the breath of life and man became a living being" (Genesis 2:7). This breath of Life which God constantly breathes into us is our spirit, which Durckheim calls "essential being," but at the same time he breathes into us

His own life as Father-Son-Holy Spirit, that is to say, our "celestial origin." The Christ reiterates this gesture the day after his resurrection, restoring creation and breathing anew on his disciples. We are not only a passive temple of the Trinitarian Presence, for we are always animated, vivified and maintained in existence by the Divine Trinity.

As it is written in Psalm 104: "You send your Breath and we are created; you withdraw your Breath and we die and return to dust." One day Durckheim took the risk to make this astonishing statement: "Our inhalation is the exhalation of God within us, and our exhalation is the inhalation of God in Himself." It is in this exchange of divine- human breath that is found the metamorphosis of human beings. We are in process of evolution and we are truly human only if we become god. There only can we be born to that which is unique within us: the person, the "Reality" of which Graf Durckheim said that it alone interested him and not experiences of liberation, for "enlightenment does not make an enlightened one"! Transformation into a person is truly the birth of the human being.

But there is only God who is truly Person and we can only become so through "participation," as Durckheim called it. The conscious sensation of the presence of God right into the intimacy of our breathing brings forth a communion-osmosis where the face of Christ becomes visible in ours, gives us existence and form, literally transfiguring us. All the saints and sages bear witness to this radiance. Without this divinization, we have no face, it is only formless chaos, "we carry the mask of the beast" said Saint Gregory of Nyssa (fourth century). This is a supreme inhabitation of a double consciousness, that of God and that of the human being; they become transparent to each other and fuse without confusion into a profound reciprocity where the person is revealed.

The "wheel of metamorphosis" never ceases to deepen and only releases its secret according to our perseverance. That is why it is crucial during its practice to take root in this context, to know the aim thanks to study of the Bible in order not to become exhausted in a technique which may lead nowhere: "letting go--giving oneself--surrendering--rebirth." The key is not repeating the words but fulfilling them. Otherwise they become fantasies getting in the way of our contact with God. Truly living what these words expressed against the background we have evoked is accomplished in the immediate presence of God, the "sensation of the Divine," according to the famous expression of the fathers.

Our consciousness is then without object or content, but remains pure, completely occupied with the experience of the reality of God, thereby becoming pure transparence. In that moment, words and all technique disappear and we are flooded with peace, joy, and love which are the three great signs that we have penetrated into the spirit or "essential being."

THE NUMINOUS

The person who lives in these depths also sees beings and things in their depths. For him, all creation becomes a place of communion with God for there is nothing which is not the expression of His glory and the receptacle of His Breath (Psalm 104). He discovers the "numinous," that superior quality which indicates to us the presence of another reality which is completely different from the one which is evident to our senses. Teilhard de Chardin calls it the "diaphany" of Being, the "Universal Smile coming from the heart of all things...the first shiver perceived from the world animated by the Incarnation of God" (The Divine Milieu), and the Fathers of the desert call it by this admirable expression: "the flame of things."

At the center of the least object is the infinite immensity which contains everything. This unity of the vision is the unity of Being and a conquest of time and space. This vision sees the infinite in the finite of things and all eternity in the passing second. This was one of Durkcheim's favorite themes and he often said that "we should look at the outside as we look within, making the outside a within," allowing us to discover that there is no exteriority, nothing is "objective" and that all is a relation of subject to subject. Before the humblest flower, we find ourselves in a relationship of "I" to "You," and can experience in a tulip the whole mystery of Being and enter into dialogue with it. This can go from the simplest sensation of Being, an ephemeral touch, to the "starry hours" and even to the great liberating experience.

The essential is to constantly exercise oneself, taking daily life as exercise; we should never lose contact with the numinous and "follow its trace everywhere, as the hunting dog follows the tracks of the game," Durckheim said, and he loved to quote the aphorism of Novalis: "Every visible surface has an invisible depth raised to a state of mystery." The Bible is so filled with this reality that Saint Augustine (fifth century) was able to say that the world and nature are a "first Bible," corresponding to Holy Scripture since they have the same Author. Both of them open onto the Christ who, after having written them, made of them his body and his face. The Logos, the incarnated Word liberates the silence of beings and of things. He gives them their deepest content and reveals their roots in the abyss of God to whom they become transparent. In visible forms, as in the words of the Bible, the Word hides and unveils itself, which is a leitmotif dear to Maximus the Confessor (seventh century).

Origen (second century) said: "The Word is present in every being, however small it may be, so that the disciples can perceive the whiteness and brilliance of the light of Truth which is everywhere." Denys the Areopagite (sixth century), one of the inspirers of Meister Eckhart, insisted that "man must unite himself with everything in order to liberate the praise of mute nature." The meaning of the world in the Bible is that it is a theophany, a manifestation of God who, in turn, offers Himself in communion with those who know how to look and contemplate. Each thing, all that exists is therefore a donation from the Invisible, opening itself on infinite horizons. This contemplation calls forth praise; since all is gift and grace, the human heart enters into thanksgiving and gratefulness.

The vision of the contemplative becomes "heliomorphous," according to Saint Gregory of Nyssa (fourth century): the light of his eyes is that of the Holy Spirit, he sees with the "eyes of the Dove" and recognizes that which is homogeneous to him, for the light which is in his eyes is the very one which flows over all things. This is the presence of the Holy Spirit which makes us "see," for It is the Beauty which attracts us in all things and calls to us through this transparence to contemplate the Word. This radiance of the Spirit which illuminates the Son penetrates our consciousness, if it opens itself to it, and gives us the sensation of God, the Silence-Source-Creator behind everything.

The person who is touched by this overwhelming experience is transformed and seized by the "cosmic mercy which inflames his heart with love for all creatures" (P. Evdokimov). Maximus the Confessor tells us that this person has attained wisdom. He is freed from all perversion and covetousness. He truly discovers a new way of being and another relationship to the world. The earth is again a paradise and human life a celestial condition.

BECOMING REAL

THE BODY THAT WE ARE

The concrete field where this immense experience of transformation takes place is our own body. It is the foundation of everything in Durckheim's work as a path and an "instrument of transcendence." It is through the body that experience is verified and finds its fulfillment. Everyone knows the famous distinction which Durckheim makes between "the body that we have" and "the body that we are." The first is an object, a possession, that which permits us to function on the exterior, a sort of prison for the soul which doesn't have much to do with it.

This is a well known duality in the West which has given birth to a certain way of seeing and treating (or mistreating!) human beings in medicine, in school and in the many ways which pretend to take care of us. "But," said Durckheim," in looking at you I do not see a body behind which I imagine a soul...It is you that I see!" In other words: I am my body. My body is my way of being there, it is my expression in the world; in it I experience my personhood and through it my personhood can live and "take shape"; consciousness of self is always physical, corporal. It means therefore that we are one, that the body is the place of initiation into the mysteries of Life and that it is called to become transparent to Being which rests in its depths so that it may bear witness to it in the world.

So the body is the path of every moment, even in the least of its gestures. Beyond the centuries of historical deviation in the West, where the human body became a garbage can for our ignorance, Durckheim helps us to rediscover the radically different vision of Christianity. The Christ introduces this concept for the first time in the history of humanity. The metaphysical meaning of the incarnation of God, which is the foundational mystery of

Christianity, rests above all else on the recognition of the metaphysical nature of corporality, which is expressed with great power in the biblical teaching of the resurrection of bodies. The body is metaphysically part of the being of man and death which destroys the body cannot completely annihilate it: "Do you not know that your body is a temple of the Holy Spirit which lives within you?" said Saint Paul, and "your bodies are members of Christ" (1 Co 6:19 and 15).

One of the great signs of verification of these teachings is this yearning which inhabits each person, this spiritual hunger which is found as much in the body as it is in the soul. In other words: the body is not an object which we have, but the physical manifestation of that which is metaphysical, beyond the physical, the visible expression of the invisible mystery of being, the exteriorization on the historical level of the inner dimension of man beyond space and time. In the Old Testament there is not even a word to express "body" as a reality separated from the rest! We are an inseparable whole: in all our aspects we are spiritual and corporal, a reciprocal and total co penetration. The juxtaposition of a body plus a soul, plus a spirit is the fruit of the original division and of our separating sin.

The path consists precisely in recovering our lost unity. According to the Tradition, which is the living commentary on the Bible, it is the whole person who is created in the image of God, that is, the human being is integrally, body-soul-spirit, in communion with God and as such "dressed with the Word and the Holy Spirit." The body itself is therefore in the image of God, in the image of the body of Christ who is God incarnate. As Saint Sophrony of Jerusalem (sixth century) said: "It is at the same time flesh was both flesh and flesh of the Word of God...for it is through Him, and not through itself that it has life." And Saint Symeon (eleventh century) does not hesitate to say: "The Spirit makes the Christ penetrate within us right to our fingertips, he penetrates our body."

The person of Christ penetrated human flesh and glorified it forever by introducing the human body into the heart of the Divine Trinity on the day of the Ascension. If therefore "it is in Christ that the body has life," it is in Him that it finds its internal principle which is spiritual. The body is the expression of the person. Both the Bible and the Tradition completely ignore the Manichean or Gnostic dualism which sees evil in the body and opposes it to spirit. And it is for the same reasons that Christianity has always been weary of both the excesses of the flesh as well as the excesses of asceticism! If it is true that on the Path I am my body, to annihilate it or escape from it is to hurt my personhood. That is why Saint Paul says: "No one has ever hated his own body" (Ephesians 5:29). The body is a "temple" but not in the manner of an external container or of a house sheltering its inhabitant: this would still be duality. The body is inhabited by God as iron is inhabited by fire.

This image is found throughout the Tradition. It is a fusion without confusion, just as the iron remains iron and the fire remains fire. It is a communion, a carnal reciprocity, a true "blending," to quote again an expression of Saint Gregory of Nyssa: "man is deified by this blending with God." This incessant transfiguration of the divine life within us is the work of the Holy Spirit and is the infinite mystery of its "kenosis" (its abnegation), of the total gift of Itself when It breathes into us the presence of the Word with whom It puts us in immediate contact at every moment. The power of its creative breath penetrates and animates our whole being and our body right into the least of its cells. The Holy Spirit has only one passion, if we can express it that way, and that is to model us into the resemblance of Christ! That is why "breathing is the great movement of Life," Durck-heim tells us, "the movement of transparence to Transcendence."

HARA

The point of departure, the place of anchoring this trans-formation in and through the body that I am, is its center of gravity, its vital center which Graf Durckheim calls with the Japanese "hara," stomach, whose fulfillment is the opening of the heart where earth and sky meet. Durckheim brought this treasure back from Japan and his book on this subject has become a masterpiece in the West. But he brought it back as an Old Testament, that is, as a promise still unfulfilled which only finds its com-pletion and ultimate meaning in the Christ. "If someone reduces "Hara" to the literal meaning of 'stomach,' he has not understood anything," says Durckheim. For "the cen-ter of man is also the incandescent center of an encounter, that of the Christ. He is the Center of every center and the Principle of every form, the Word through which everything subsist, the One who unites earth and sky...Man is therefore in his center there where he feels himself one with Christ and hears his call as the inner master.

His whole life then rises out of the Christ..." (Dialogue on the Path of Initiation). Christianity has, unfortunately, lost long ago the key to the reading of the most signifi-cant biblical texts and to the most ancient iconography related to "Hara." References to it are nevertheless eve-rywhere omnipresent as much in the Old Testament as in the New Testament, and in Christian icons and sculp-tures. Durckheim offers us several reproductions in his book, including a marvelous byzantine Christ of the sixth century with a protuberant Hara. Only the saints or true spiritual persons, those who have experienced this reali-ty, still know what this is about and can interpret its message. Durckheim has done an enormous work of deciphering. "The moment has come to rediscover in the great tradition of primitive Christianity its treasure buried in initiatory knowledge and experiential wisdom."

The Bible is filled with the necessity of earthly rooting. One of the most extraordinary texts on this subject is the parable of the sower (Matthew 13, Mark 4, Luke 8), where Jesus gives an anthropology of the person of prayer and shows us how nothing happens in the person who has no depth of earth nor roots in himself. These are dazzling expressions to say in biblical language what "Hara" is. This experiential language runs throughout the parable and makes us feels instantly what it is talking about. In another passage, Jesus compares man to a house: "he dug, he went deep and placed the foundations on a rock" (Luke 7:48). Christ returns constantly to this reality in many ways.

As a good Semite, Saint Paul uses the same realistic and carnal language, where the body is never left out of the Way. "Be rooted and founded in love, and you will receive the power to understand...and you will enter through your depth into the Depth of God" (Ephesians 3:17-19). Saint Gregory Palamas (fourteenth century) and other Fathers of the Philokalia state that the navel must be our foundation for the "law of my God is in the middle of my stomach." These are not recopies but simply honest expressions of the movement of Incarnation which transforms the innards of human beings into the matrix of life. In the Old Testament the words which recur most often to describe "Hara" are translated as "mercy," which does not render very well the reality in question: the Hebrew "rehem" means matrix, the entrails of love. But other expressions are frequently used such as "rock, citadel, refuge, rampart, shield, tower, shelter, cornerstone, rib, power..." which refer to the center of man according to the context and, of course, according to the level of consciousness with which we approach the reading. It is always important that the reading be "carnal" or incarnated.

That is where the dynamism of the whole Bible is found: "God comes to experience man so that man can experience God" (Saint Athanasius, sixth century); the Word always wants to become flesh. For a true Semite, verbal abstraction is a scandal and a betrayal; the word ("dabar" in Hebrew) expresses the depth of things. For him, "the corporal criteria is superior to all psychological criteria because, simple and completely objective, it is not subject to interpretations and errors whose true value and nature only becoming teaches" (Anthony Bloom). In conclusion, I would willingly place Graf Durckheim under the patronage of Saint Thomas, the doubting apostle, who refused to believe in Christ resurrected as long as he had not placed his fingers and hands into the wounds. Christ appeared to him and allowed him to do so, but added: "Blessed are those who will believe without having seen!" (John 20:24-29). "To see" is still to maintain a distance, to objectify, to leave the Christ on the exterior. And the wish of Saint Thomas is fulfilled beyond all his desires, for "the Kingdom of God is within you" -- "abide in me as I abide in you" (John 15).

From then on faith gives primacy to experience. After his earthly mission, Jesus did not say to his disciples: "You will think of me" but: "Touch me!" and "He breathed upon them" (Luke 24:39 and John 20:22). Christ living within us touches us completely, constantly and we touch him, right into the intimacy of our breath. He breathes within us: "Flesh of my flesh, blood of my blood!" cries out Gregory, and we are "blessed" because now "we can feel everything in God" (Saint Isaac the Syrian, sixth century).

BECOMING REAL

THE WHEEL OF TRANSFORMATION

by Theodore J. Nottingham

"The first and most vital practice in everyday life is to learn effectively to value those moments in which we are touched by something hitherto undreamt of."

The German psychotherapist and spiritual master, Karlfried Graf Durckheim died in the winter of 1988 at the age of ninety-two. The inner practice which he developed over his many years of study, travel and experience offers to contemporary seekers a way of radical transformation.

Combining the insights and practices of Zen Buddhism with depth psychology and Christian mysticism, he has created a potent, practical way of inner work which thousands have undertaken. Durckheim begins his teaching by focusing on our rare moments of higher consciousness, those numinous experiences which he names "privileged moments" and "life's starry hours." These are unforgettable times when something greater than our usual awareness breaks through and floods us with unaccountable serenity, joy, or certainty. Such experiences call us toward a new way of living and initiate us into a different view of reality. Mystics, philosophers, saints, and esotericists of all times have pointed to these radiant moments as proof that we are meant to be more than we seem to be. These events have opened our eyes to the higher influences present in our world.

Many teachings have attempted to bring us to a near continual experience of this higher consciousness, but they all seem to suffer a similar fate. Almost as soon as these teachings have been transmitted, they become rigid and dogmatic, and the spirit gives way to the letter. Durckheim's method begins and ends with the individual on his or her unique path. He offers no theory, no cosmology, no religious philosophy. He merely tells us in the magnificent simplicity of eastern sages that each moment is the best of opportunities for working on oneself, and he provides us with a process for the expansion of consciousness which he calls the Wheel of Metamorphosis. These are inner disciplines which each must apply to himself or herself. Verification and understanding come out of lived experience.
Durckheim warns us that this practice must be done continuously with concentrated awareness or it will lead nowhere. The Wheel of Metamorphosis consists of three stages and five steps:

Stage 1-- all that is contrary to essential being must be relinquished.
step 1: the practice of critical watchfulness
step 2: the letting go of all that stands in the way of new becoming

Stage 2-- that which has been relinquished must be dissolved in transcendent Being which absorbs and recreates us.
step 3: union with transcendent Being
step 4: new becoming in accordance with the inner image which has arisen from transcendent Being

Stage 3-- the newly formed core must be recognized and

personal responsibility taken for its growth.

step 5: practicing this new form on a daily basis through critical watchfulness which leads us back to step one of the process

In this linear expression of the wheel, it may appear difficult to capture the holistic context in which these changes occur. But the key to this process lies in the fact that each step contains all the others and only has meaning within the context of the continuous revolution of the wheel. We are dealing with the cyclic movement of a spiral: critical watchfulness--letting go--union--new becoming generate ceaseless transformation.

Durckheim names this inner practice "self-becoming." The term suggests a dynamic, natural movement which rises out of who we are, just as the image of the flower is contained in its seed. Clearly, intense effort remains a vital part of the journey, but Durckheim's teaching is grounded in natural processes rooted in our earth center, the place within where we are constantly created by cosmic life-forces and which the Japanese call "hara."

For Durckheim, higher consciousness --which he names transcendent or divine Being-- seeks to manifest itself through our bodily presence. This life-force actively seeks to become conscious of itself through our awakening to our essential nature. All of the exercises, practices and insights which Durckheim offers us are meant to render us "transparent to transcendent Being." A conscious being is one through whom the divine life radiates. The personality has been made entirely permeable and obedient to essence, the subconscious has been cleansed and liberated, and the way is cleared for our higher centers to express themselves through our state of openness, receptivity, and presence in the moment.

This work on oneself is not centered on self for the sake of self. Durckheim has a much wider panorama in view.

BECOMING REAL

Our efforts are meant to prepare us to reach a state where life in the service of transcendent Being becomes second nature. In discovering our own essential self, we participate in the manifestation of what can only be described as divine, the source of mercy, compassion, and conscious love. Such a possibility requires work on all parts of our nature. But Durckheim is especially insistent on the body as a key to breaking through to a greater consciousness. "*Whenever a wrong posture has become deeply ingrained it blocks the redeeming, renewing and preserving forces that arise from the depths of Being.*"

Durckheim respects it as an expression of transcendent Being in a particular form and calls upon us to seek our right center of gravity within it. This requires work on posture, tension, and breathing. The primary practice to achieve such centering is meditation. This fundamental exercise, however, is not to be confused with the various methods used in our New Age culture. Durckheim tells us that "*the purpose of correct practice is not to bring man to a state of tranquility but to keep him in a condition of constant watchfulness and prevent him from coming to a standstill on the Way.*"

The energy of attention becomes a vital resource for transformation. Moreover, the fundamental effort of divided attention found in the teachings of the Fourth Way and of eastern Christianity is central to Durckheim's inner practice: "*Without the attention that collects the whole person--so that he is at the same time focused within himself and turned towards the object--no meditation is possible.*"

This continuous awareness is maintained outside of meditation as well, and is focused on our usual behavior so as to dissolve that which blocks the possibility of radiating a vaster consciousness. Durckheim names it "critical watchfulness" which means continual inner awareness of our behavior, in other words, self-observation.

This relentless effort is meant to lead to a growth of consciousness that provides us with a new sensitivity enabling us to perceive all deviations from our correct center. Durckheim identifies this center as a state wherein a person moves continuously toward his innermost nature. It is not a place but our driving force calling us home. From this center we are able to acquire a clear sense of inner direction, and above all, a "*self-confidence that is independent of the world's praise or blame.*" Without this center, we are the plaything of inner and outer forces.

"*Practice on ourselves, in the physical and spiritual sense, is always of two kinds. It involves both the pulling-down of everything that stands in the way of our contact with Divine Being, and the building-up of a 'form' which, by remaining accessible to its inner life, preserves this contact and affirms it in every activity in the world.*"

Durckheim insists that if we have become conscious of our essence, we have become conscious of our union with transcendence. But to achieve this, we need to have the courage to meet the unknown, and to "*endure the mystery that cannot be conceptually comprehended--in short, to pause and inwardly dwell in that to which we are all too unaccustomed -- the radiance of Divine Being.*" Durckheim calls upon us to risk over and over again all that we think we have understood, all that we hold onto as security.

Durckheim deals with the dominance of our artificial personality through the psycho-physical process of "letting go." His long years of study in Zen Buddhism, including eight years with Zen masters in Japan, resulted in his discovery of the unquestionable link between psychological attitudes and bodily tensions. To be released

from our misconceptions and buffers is not merely a
mental effort but requires dissolving the physical knots
and distorted postures which express these attitudes.
Clenched jaws, cramped stomachs, raised shoulders all
keep us outside of the realm of essence which is the only
threshold to our true becoming. Letting go also means
*"forsaking the brilliance of the rational mind and enter-
ing the semi-darkness of another form of consciousness."*

The tyranny of the intellectual center and of a cultural
worldview reduced to the surface of the five senses can
be a powerful barrier to the reception of divine inspiration.

*"By letting go in the right way, we learn to 'let in' and 'let
happen' that which, in spite of all our ideas, projections,
desires and prejudices, meets us directly in the shape of
the world and comes from the constantly stirring essential being within."*

Durckheim sought to awaken people to their higher
selves and to the deeper dimensions of reality. As a mas-
terful teacher, he only present a partial picture of a state
of being that cannot be expressed in words. His ultimate
purpose is to serve as a signpost pointing in the direction
of that which is within every one of us and which we
must each discover for ourselves.